THE
MONEY
TEAM

*Twenty-four Financial Experts Show You
How To Weave A Personal Safety Net*

*Complied and edited by
Grant Sylvester
and
John Millyard*

MONEY JAR PUBLISHING
Publishers of:
The Money Jar
The Money Gap

MONEY JAR Publishing

This publication attempts to provide accurate and authoritative information as to its subject. It should be understood that the publisher is not offering legal, accounting or other professional services. Readers wishing to act upon suggestions in this publication should first seek the expert advice of an appropriate competent professional.

OTHER BOOKS BY MONEY JAR PUBLISHING:
The Money Jar
The Money Gap

Canadian Cataloguing in Publication Data

Main entry under title:
The money team: 24 financial experts show you how to weave a personal safety net

ISBN 0-9695889-3-3

1. Finance, Personal. 2. Financial security. I. Millyard, John. II Sylvester, Grant.

HGI79.M664 1998   332.024'01   C98-931138-4

Typesetting & design: *JDM ASSOCIATES*, Willowdale, ON
Cover design: *Willem Hart.*
Printed and bound in Canada

MONEY JAR Publishing
642 Sheppard Ave. E., Suite 1711
Willowdale, ON
CANADA M2K 1B9
Tel. & fax: (416) 223-7312
E-mail: millyard@home.com

CONTENTS

CONTENTS . . . . . . *continued*

NOTE

The statements and statistics contained herein are based on material believed to be reliable but the publisher cannot guarantee that they are accurate or complete.

This compilation of chapters is editorial material provided by various Money Concepts financial planners as identified in each chapter, and is for informational purposes only. All the authors are registered to deal in mutual funds and life insurance. Particular investments or planning strategies are not necessarily suitable for everyone, and should be evaluated relative to each individual's objectives in consultation with their financial advisors.

Graphics, charts, statistical and tabular material is provided by the authors unless otherwise noted in the text.

The Money Concepts organization includes Money Concepts (Canada) Limited, Money Concepts Group Capital Corp. and National Financial Marketing Services Insurance Agency Inc.

Mutual funds are sold by prospectus only. The simplified prospectus contains important information that you should read carefully before investing. You may obtain a copy from your vendor or the appropriate fund company.

IN MEMORY
OF
GRANT SYLVESTER

Harvey

May you enjoy
Health, Wealth
&
Happiness

Allan
Jan/2001

Foreword

By Grant D. Sylvester, CLU, CFP, RFP

I have written two books about personal financial planning, the latter with my son, Rob, the president of our company, Money Concepts (Canada) Limited. When our publisher approached me to write a third, I pondered the idea one weekend as I baked lazily in the sun on our cottage dock. Do I have the time, I wondered? Are there other things I want to focus on to help guide our company's rapid, almost phenomenal, growth? In fact, why me at all? There are so many other well-qualified financial professionals around these days, many of them right in our own company. For a second I marvelled at the huge pool of planning expertise at Money Concepts, especially considering our more-than-modest beginnings back in April 1985.

That line of thought led directly to this book. Why pick the brains of just one financial advisor, I thought, when you have 24 of the best at your fingertips. (We really have many more than 24 of the best at Money Concepts, but I had to draw the line somewhere unless I wanted to write an encyclopaedia. It was a most difficult task to narrow down our list of contributors to form this elite MONEY TEAM.)

At Money Concepts we are very proud of, and diligently maintain the quality of, our associates. There are several reasons for the high calibre of people operating under the Money Concepts banner. First, we place a premium on attracting and selecting franchise presidents and account executives with the highest professional skills and level of academic education. All of them are people with exceptional talent, and many have postgraduate degrees.

No less important is their high level of personal ethics. They are right at home with a demanding code of business ethics.

Another reason for the high standards of Money Concepts affiliates is the pre-eminent excellence of the comprehensive training program they must undertake. This mandatory program extends for eight months and incorporates field training along with classroom work. It is followed by institutional training in the various financial services sectors involved in the planning process, such as mutual funds or insurance. Everybody representing the company also is encouraged to qualify for an industry-wide planning designation that reflects their competence.

Such training, I should point out, is not just undertaken when they join the company. It continues throughout every representative's career.

We use a standard system, but it allows for individuality and personal specialization

Training in the Money Concepts' system is comprehensive and vital to a representative's success, but it still leaves a lot of room for individuality and entrepreneurial applications. While every company team member is provided with the same financial planning system, there is ample room for each of them to follow their own inclinations and employ their own special abilities. Some have added to the system to embellish it in their particular area of interest. Others focus their planning skills on specific demographic or age groups. Some develop highly specialized professional expertise, perhaps in risk management, will planning, tax planning, estate planning or educational planning.

The Money Concepts planning system itself is centred on a comprehensive, computerized approach. It incorporates some fundamental principles such as encouraging representatives to establish long-term, trusting relationships with people in their communities, and to become known as someone who does a more-than-capable professional job for clients. This usually results in a remarkable number of personal referrals to new business.

The Money Concepts' system considers each client as an individual with specific wants and needs, and usually different priorities or levels of risk tolerance. A planner's job starts with a thorough assessment of those needs (along with the client), then proceeds by helping the client set priorities and establish long-term goals. When goals are agreed upon, the next step is a written plan. This is really an analysis of the information the client provides and a determination how to maximize the client's financial resources to get what they want.

Money Concepts planners invest many hours in developing financial plans for clients without the expectation of immediate rewards. They know that if they provide the very best face-to-face financial planning for prospective clients—without fee or compensation—they will eventually earn clients' trust. Planners will then be rewarded if clients decide to implement their plans with various financial products that the planners suggest. Money Concepts tries to give before receiving. It's like the old adage that suggests you cast your bread upon the water and someday it will come back a hundred-fold.

Educational seminars are part of the Money Concepts' system that was perfected here in Canada. Seminars comprise the backbone of establishing a credible presence in the communities our planners serve. We also provide educational pamphlets, newsletters, brochures and bulletins to people looking for answers to their money-management questions. Clients learn that they really have to do their own financial planning, but they usually need a little bit of help. Hence the Money Concepts slogan: *You must do it yourself and you can't do it alone.*

The plan and its implementation is not the end of the road in the extensive planning process. Our planners keep in touch with their clients, and are trained to routinely review their financial plans and to make suggestion for fine-tuning, if needed.

Our planners are objective because they are free to suggest financial products from the entire marketplace

---

One of the reasons the Money Concepts' system works is because it provides objective, independent advice and recommendations to clients. Planners are free to select, from the marketplace, the companies, financial products and services that best meet clients' needs. The company does not have financial products of its own and is not bound to any supplier firms or industry sectors.

The sum of all this—people plus training plus systems—is the reason that Money Concepts has not just survived, but thrived. In the spring of 1998, the company became a teenager and celebrated its 13th birthday. We look upon this milestone as the company's coming of age—we have moved through its infancy, developed more fully in adolescence and now are approaching adulthood.

Money Concepts is in the forefront of Canadian mutual fund dealers

I think it's quite a story. Just 14 years previous, the sum total of the Money Concepts staff was two. Today, there are nearly 100 offices across Canada in eight of the 10 provinces. There are more than 375 president/owners and account executives and a support staff of almost 200 between home office and the franchises. That's more than 500 people. We are doing our part to create jobs in Canada.

Money Concepts' business mission is to help middle-income Canadians with financial planning. As a result, we are very much involved with clients' wealth-creation plans, their retirement-income planning, the education of their children and the establishment of emergency and opportunity funds. We allot a major role to the area of risk management— helping clients to protect themselves and their families in the event of premature death, disability, liability coverages and long-term healthcare during the advancing years. We are also involved with tax planning, will planning and estate planning.

Because we have been dealing extensively with the baby-boom generation, much of our work has been in retirement planning. Mutual funds have been an integral part of this process, and Money Concepts now is among the forefront of Canadian mutual fund dealers. Our mutual fund dealership arm, Money Concepts Group Capital Corporation, has shown a dramatic increase since 1987 when we first offered these products to implement financial plans. Just 12 years later we have about $2 billion in fund assets under administration. We consider that phenomenal growth.

I believe the next two decades are going to be golden years for financial services. Low interest rates, baby-boomer savings that will seek solid investment returns and a strong, growing economy will all contribute.

There will be an enormous increase in the number of financial planners

There will be an enormous increase in the number of financial planners and financial advisors operating through various types of financial institutions. Our company's financial planners will be on the crest of this wave, leading clients of all ages and incomes towards financial peace of mind.

But now it's time to introduce you to 24 financial planners who have already developed impeccable credentials helping clients solve their money management problems. They are among the finest people I have ever been associated with in business. I hope their stories will make you realize that your financial problems are not insurmountable–and that most problems are opportunities in disguise.

The late GRANT D. SYLVESTER was chairman, CEO and co-founder of Money Concepts (Canada) Limited.

1

Extra Mortgage Payments Could be a Big Mistake

By Ron Lindsay Brown, CFP

*O*ne of the biggest myths about financial management—and one extremely difficult to overcome—is that you'll be financially secure when you finally pay down your mortgage.

This notion has been handed down for many decades—particularly from the Great Depression era—and goes hand in hand with the nonsense that your home is your greatest investment. You'll never land in the poorhouse, the assumption goes, if you don't have any mortgage payments to make.

In the 1920s and '30s, and for many, even through to the '50s, it took every cent most families earned just to cover the essentials of food, shelter and clothing. Some of us can remember that far back, when a vacation was rare, if ever, and the accumulation of financial assets was the stuff of dreams. It was a great day indeed when the family home was finally paid for. I once attended a mortgage-burning party—a more common celebration years ago than now.

Today most Canadians live well beyond that kind of marginal existence. Yet, by making mortgage prepayments, they often pass up an excellent opportunity to accumulate wealth. They are beset by an almost organic fear that they have to race to pay off their home before it's somehow suddenly snatched away from them. The marketing departments and lending officers of banks and other lending institutions aid and abet that mindset.

Accelerating home payments can cost you liquidity

This very means of trying to avoid poverty has had the opposite effect on many Canadians—because larger-than-necessary mortgage payments can eat up your cash, leaving no cushion for emergencies. In the severe recession of 1981–82, at least 200 families in Windsor, Ontario, lost their homes, according to the *Windsor Star*. There was plenty of equity available in a substantial number of these situations (equity being the difference between current home value and the [lower] balance on the mortgage). But nobody was buying houses even though prices had become depressed. You couldn't sell your home to get your hands on the equity. In addition, employment prospects were bleak. If you were unemployed and had exhausted employment insurance benefits, you could not get a loan to help you survive the recession. Distressed homeowners had nowhere to turn. Foreclosure was the result. They certainly couldn't sever a couple of rooms or the backyard pool and sell them with the hope of buying them back when prosperity returned. The equity they had accumulated over the years was gone forever.

Others in Windsor wisely had been gathering financial assets. It was a different story for them. They could tap into RRSPs or other savings and investments for the emergency cash to see them through the tough times. One client of mine saved both his gas station business and his home with proceeds from his RRSPs. Eating into RRSPs is not the recommended approach to building wealth, but there is a time and place for everything.

An example of liquidity (in)action

Fred and Mae were in their late 40s when they came to see me early in 1997. They complained of being cash-strapped and not being able to afford their oldest child's university tuition that fall. Also, they had to make some overdue home renovations. Short-term debts exceeded their savings (a group RRSP) by a ratio of almost three to one. They were sliding further into debt to the tune of $300 per month. They feared they would never be able to put away a financial nest egg to augment Fred's pension in retirement.

This was a classic case of lack of liquidity and flexibility, and it is typical of the financial circumstances of too many Canadians. Because of their adherence to the pay-down-mortgage-fast myth, they couldn't see the forest for the trees. There was good news right in front of their noses, but they needed somebody experienced in money management to point it out to them.

Between them, Fred and Mae had take-home pay of about $60,000 a year. They were average spenders. They owed only $54,000 on a home valued at $150,000. What was pinning them down and squeezing the financial life out of them was a very hefty mortgage prepayment scheme, thanks to the generous compliance of their bank that never did a proper cash-flow analysis or any other serious financial planning when setting up the scheme. (Later in this chapter we'll look at how mortgage prepayment or accelerated payments are far better for the bank and its lending officers than they are for you, the client.)

Although the balance of their home loan was only $54,000, they were making weekly payments of $1,806 a month! Little wonder they couldn't build an emergency fund apart from a small group RRSP. Little wonder they found it impossible to make RRSP contributions or afford the renovations to the house.

What I suggested to Fred and Mae was, well, nothing short of revolutionary, at least for them. The first step was a new 25-year consolidation mortgage of $82,000. This allowed them to pay off an annoying $500-a-month short-term loan and two other, smaller but nagging, obligations. Now they pay only the minimum monthly mortgage payment instead of four loan payments. This freed up $1,660 a month to apply to new priorities.

Next, we jump-started their long-term capital accumulation with a $13,500 spousal RRSP contribution loan (Fred had lots of unused RRSP contribution room). Partly as a result of this, Fred received a hefty $7,400 tax refund later in the year.

We reallocated some of the $1,600 monthly surplus from the refinancing in the following way:

Repayment spousal RRSP loan (over five years)	$263
Regular RRSP contributions	$300
Tuition fund build-up (no-load money-market fund)	$400
House fund (renovations)	$300
Who-cares fund (mad money)	$97
TOTAL	*$1,360*

From sliding further into debt at about $300 a month to a balanced budget, perhaps even a small surplus: a pretty positive and satisfying swing.

Once college days are behind them and home renovations are completed, Fred and Mae will have a lot more to pump into long-term savings. If they follow through with their plan and Fred takes early retirement, they'll have enough capital to generate income to cover the remaining mortgage payments plus an extra $10,000 to $15,000 yearly in spending money.

A year later during our annual financial plan review, Fred told me everything was going forward pretty much as planned. The tuition money is there for every semester, the RRSP contributions are being made, and everything else seems to be getting done.

More importantly, Fred and Mae's savings would give them flexibility during a possible financial crisis, especially now that they have no short-term debt. They would be in a position to instantly slash about $1,100 from monthly commitments without taking a major hit to their lifestyle. This new liquidity and flexibility has given the family a more confident and optimistic view of the future.

Truth in lending!!

It can be terribly intimidating when, suggesting quicker and cheaper ways to pay, mortgage lenders often throw out a figure such as $100,000 or more in the total interest cost you'll have to pay over the full amortization period of the mortgage. But I consider it is a deceitful exercise on their part. And the lenders' approach is made more credible by what you probably have heard from your friends, their parents, your parents and their parents.

By always showing just one side of the mortgage equation, the banks are leading you up the garden path. For you that path often leads to financial stress. For them, it usually leads to greater profitability. Like lemmings, millions of Canadian homebuyers follow the lenders' advice as if it were gospel. They take a short amortization period, go long on the term (five or seven years) and prepay through weekly or biweekly plans.

Prepaying for shelter (accelerating your mortgage payments beyond what is needed) can be very expensive. If you do that you could miss a lot of exciting financial opportunities. To judge for yourself, you should accumulate all the facts about the misunderstood process of home financing.

The picture that lenders—banks, credit unions, trust and life-insurance companies— want indelibly framed in your mind is the long-term total interest cost. For instance, if you take out a $100,000 mortgage at 7%, at the end of 25 years you will have paid a total of $108,000 in interest. Viewed out of context, the thought of paying twice for your home is ugly at best.

What the lenders don't tell you is that if the history of the past 30 years repeats itself, your $100,000 home will be worth anywhere between $500,000 and $800,000 in 25 years. Much depends, of course, on where you live, the type of house you have and the average rate of inflation. Your home is really a leveraged investment: you use the bank's money, interest notwithstanding, to buy an appreciating asset. When you eventually sell the property, you don't share the profit with the bank or anyone else—even the tax department.

The right way to save interest costs

Another thing lenders don't tell you is the right way to save on total interest cost. Their way is to present you with a table showing annual lump-sum payments of, say, $5,000, and how that will reduce your 25 years of payments to about 11 years. This can cut your total interest cost by about 60%.

Yet, their own studies demonstrate that you can effect a substantial reduction of your interest cost just by going short on the term. In other words, instead of taking a five- or seven-year term (the ones the banks promote) with a locked-in interest rate, use a six-month or one-year term.

In the mid 1990s, the Bank of Montreal released a study that showed impressive interest-cost savings in two out of three five-year periods for homebuyers who used the one-year term. The study went back as far as the early 1980s. It used the average price of a home back then and a 25% down payment. It found that in the first five-year period, a series of five one-year mortgages saved more than $28,000 compared to a single five-year mortgage using the locked-in 1981 rate. Of course, this was a period of sharply declining rates.

But what about more normal circumstances? In a period of flat or stable interest rates, the one-year mortgage saved $11,000 in interest compared to the five-year term. And, in a five-year period of increasing interest rates, the short-term broke even with the five-year.

It is critical to note that during the past 50 years, interest rates have been virtually flat or declining most of the time!

A home is a lifestyle decision, not an investment

I am sure you realize by now that I do not subscribe to the myth that your home is your greatest investment. The liquidity issue alone would be enough to scare a business person away from this proposition. Furthermore, the average, annual, compound return of residential real estate (without maintenance and repairs factored in) is about equal to that of treasury bills, the least risky and, therefore, least productive alternative investment vehicle. Apply maintenance and repair costs and it becomes an even less appealing business proposition.

Compare that to careful investment in mutual funds instead of in your home. In 1983, the average house price in Toronto was approximately $100,000, according to the Toronto Real Estate Board. It had merely doubled 13 years later. A $100,000 investment in Templeton Growth Fund grew to more than $500,000 during the same period. That's five times your money in 13 years compared to merely twice as much. A no-brainer as far as I am concerned.

Factor taxation into the mix

Let's add another, exciting, element to financing a home. Suppose you could afford that extra $5,000 a year that the bank would like you to plunk down to accelerate mortgage payments. Doing it the bank's way you'd have to earn about $8,500 gross, then pay tax of about $3,500, leaving the $5,000 net you need (using a middle-range marginal tax rate of 40%). On the other hand, if (there are almost always some "if"s in this business) you had the contribution room in your RRSP for that $5,000, and if you made that contribution, your net cost each year would be $3,000, not $8,500. This translates to $250 per month net after tax and it seems to me that's a lot easier to handle than $708 a month.

But take this thought further down the road to that magic moment in 11 years when the bank's method would anoint you mortgage free. You would have paid almost $38,000 in interest—a very expensive 11 years. To a large extent this is because mortgage lenders get the majority of their interest back in the early years of your payments.

It might be more distressing to think about what you would have given up during this period: $5,000 a year into your RRSP is a total investment of $33,000 ($55,000 minus $22,000 in tax savings). Some 11 years later that $33,000 would be worth more than $115,000, assuming an average annual compound return of 12% through good mutual funds. The Toronto Stock Exchange (TSE) 300 index has averaged a little more than 11% during the past 50 years, according to Amdex Associates Inc.

If you used the RRSP method, you'd still own your home with perhaps tens of thousands of dollars in equity added. You'd still have another 14 years of mortgage payments to make, but the $115,000 (and still growing) RRSP would be like an insurance policy to make certain those payments can be made. All the while you have been building a very large stake in your ultimate financial independence.

Perhaps in your case we might be talking about only $1,000 in extra mortgage principal payments each year, not $5,000, but the principle is the same: either it's pay yourself toward greater financial security, or pay the bank and Revenue Canada.

Why do they do it?

It's not hard to understand why the banks promote extra principal pre-payment and locking up a long-term rate—just put yourself in their shoes as a lender:

Suppose you loaned $10,000 to a friend or relative to buy a car. More often than not, though you might know a lot about that person and trust them, you'd have to accept the possibility that you'd never get back the entire sum— perhaps because of illness, loss of job, personal problems or even death. This is why institutional lenders promote loan payment insurance (it also is another source of revenue for them). If your borrower pays you a high rate of interest, you'll feel good. If the borrower comes in with a lump-sum prepayment once in a while, you'll feel even better. The combined effect of accelerated payments and higher interest payments increases your cash flow and, at the same time, reduces your risk of losing the original $10,000. You would also receive those accelerated payments in current dollars rather than later on after inflation has eaten away at their purchasing power.

To put it bluntly, financial instituions are not interested in enhancing your personal financial well-being. Their mandate is to increase cash flow and maintain a healthy balance sheet for their stockholders, for financial analysts and for bank examiners. The loan/loss or risk profile of all accounts is crucial to valuation of the bank as a healthy business.

Wouldn't you assume it's natural, then, that bank lending officers who collect the most amount of interest and principal might have a better career path than those who don't. I learned recently about a bank mortgage officer who advised the short-term and long-amortization method to all of his customers. He lost his position in a few months.

Ron's rules for home financing

♦ Make the absolute minimum down payment on your mortgage with the longest possible amortization period.

♦ Take the shortest term the lender will offer, e.g. six-month or one-year open or convertible (the conversion option may console the panicky among us who would otherwise become upset if there was a short-term, upward spike in interest rates).

♦ Make minimum monthly payments–take your sweet time paying off what may be the only leveraged investment you'll ever make.

♦ Most importantly, take the difference each year between this method and the bank's method, and invest it–especially in your RRSP.

RON LINDSAY BROWN is president of the Money Concepts Financial Planning Centre that he opened in 1986 in Windsor, Ontario. Ron has achieved the Certified Financial Planner (CFP) designation and has completed the Canadian Securities Course, the Branch Manager's exam, the Canadian Mutual Funds Course and the Life Underwriter's Training Program, Levels I and II. In a prior career, Ron was a broadcast journalist for 19 years, including eight years with the CBC. Ron and his wife, Sandra, have two sons and two grandsons. All share a passion for sports.

Ron may be reached by telephone at 519-944-4232, by fax at 519-944-3983 and by e-mail at rbrown@moneyconcepts.ca.

2

It's Never Too Late to Secure Financial Peace of Mind

By Stephen J. Defalco, BA

Are you retired and your income stream is drying up? Are you soon to retire and you have left it too long to build up a sizeable retirement fund? You can improve your income situation and financial peace of mind if you act promptly and judiciously, even if you are age 65 or beyond 80.

Many older, or retired, investors are faced with a significantly reduced income because of changing investment circumstances in recent years. Since the early 1980s, when interest rates hit a sky-high peak of around 14% annually, fixed rates of interest from guaranteed investment certificates (GICs) have slid steadily downward. Today in the late 1990s, rates for a one-year GIC are around 5% per annum. If you depend on this type of retirement income alone, you could be living on half or less of what you used to receive.

Other factors are affecting the yield from fixed-income investments. Governments worldwide and especially in Canada have instituted strong deficit-reduction programs during the past five-plus years. In 1998 for the first time in recent memory, Canada will be close to balancing its federal budget. It might, in fact, even experience a surplus. As a result, the government is borrowing less money to manage the country's finances, and the reduced demand has pushed interest rates downward. This trend is expected to endure for some time with voting-generations-to-come expected to insist on such continuing fiscal responsibility. Significantly higher interest rates are out of sight far beyond the average investment horizon.

At the same time we have already begun to feel the growing impact of the baby boomer population bulge on the investment environment. Many of the early baby boomers—now in their early 50s—recognize that if they want to retire comfortably in 12 to 15 years, they need to secure a good rate of return from both their RRSP and non-registered investments. Otherwise they won't have adequate funds to retire. They are pouring huge numbers of dollars into investments and at the same time the demand for borrowing is declining. This adds to the downward pressure on interest rates.

Interest-rate income down 64%

To get an idea of the impact on investors, consider a person with a retirement pool of $300,000. In 1981 this would have generated $42,000 in yearly interest income. In 1998, this same investor only generates $15,000. This is a real decline of $27,000 a year—64% less income compared to 1981. This example disregards the effect of inflation and tax over the time period, but suffice it to say, this investor has significantly less money to live on.

I witnessed this phenomenon first hand; for five years starting in the late 1980s I oversaw some investments on behalf of an ailing family member. My relative was on a fixed income from a pension that was not indexed so he relied on extra interest income from the investments to supplement his needs. During the five years to the early '90s, when unfortunately he passed away, his yearly interest income sank like a stone.

To compensate for this kind of reduced investment return, many investors in recent years have shifted their strategy to hold some growth investments— usually common stocks or equity mutual funds—to build their retirement funds faster or to achieve a better annual income. The conventional wisdom is to expect higher rates of return (based mainly on growth) over a long-term time horizon that allows economic cycles to run their courses. It has been amply demonstrated that over time, growth-type (equity) investments historically outperform fixed-income investments by a reasonably wide margin. In Canada for the 48-year period from 1950 to 1998, equity investments returned an average of about 11% annually, while fixed-income investments, such as GICs or bonds, returned closer to 8% yearly.

The 3% difference during this 48-year period has meant that growth investments on a compounded basis have far exceeded fixed income types. For example, if you had invested $1,000 for that length of time at 11%, you'd have ended up with $20,165 compared to the $9,057 that an 8% yield would have provided.

The following table shows the growth and average yield from different types of investments for the 48-year period January 1950 to June 1998:

TYPE OF INVESTMENT	$ GROWTH	AVERAGE YIELD
Inflation (CPI)	$748	4.2%
90-day T-bills	2,032	6.4
Scotia McL. Long-Term Bond Index	3,506	7.6
5-year GIC	3,865	7.8
TSE 300 total return index	17,065	11.2
US total return index	54,363	13.9
US small stock total return	$71,712	14.5%

The amounts are in Canadian dollars and show the average return over 47 years for the seven types of investments, for Canadian investors. **Source: Andex Associates Inc.**

There is little doubt today that a mature investor over 65 or 70 or even 80 years of age must have some growth investments in the portfolio, even if the investor's personal time frame does not appear to be long term.

In the past many investors and advisors used a general approach to determine what proportions of fixed-income versus growth holdings should be in a portfolio at certain points in their lives. This "rule of thumb" was: subtract your age from 100% and the resulting proportion should be placed in growth (or equity) holdings. So a 70-year-old investor should have 70% in fixed-income or GIC type holdings and 30% in growth type investments. This was considered a conservative approach designed to minimize risk for the mature investor, assuming that equities represent higher risk than fixed-income instruments.

It's an approach that would still be acceptable if fixed-income investments today could earn near the 10% range. With rates currently hovering around 5% yearly, this approach is outdated.

Living longer costs more

Another element to factor into the catch-up equation is longevity. As recently as the early 1980s, a man typically lived until his early 70s and a woman to her late 70s. This translates to a man retiring at 65 likely living only another seven years or so, and a woman enjoying 10 or 11 years more.

Their retirement funds had to provide income only for a decade or so after they stopped working.

During the past several decades, advancements in medical science and nutrition, along with an awareness that people must take better care of themselves, have stimulated an increase in the average life expectancy to late 70s for men and early 80s for women. This results in both a good-news and a bad-news scenario.

The good news of course is that our lives are prolonged and we are able to enjoy family and friends longer, and may be able to travel or indulge in favourite recreations for an extended time.

The bad news is that living longer costs a lot more. We must ensure that we don't outlast our retirement funds. With fixed-income reduced because of minimal interest rates, the argument is even stronger for a significant growth component in our investment portfolio, regardless of age.

The plight of some of my clients illustrates this fact. One of them (we'll call him Harry) faced a serious dilemma. He was an elderly parent in his early 80s, in reasonably good health apart from needing some slight nursing care. He entered a retirement home several years ago. At the time, Harry had about $400,000 in non-registered (non-RRSP) investments paying him interest at 9% yearly over a five-year term. This generated $36,000 per year in income, and along with a small pension plus old age security (OAS) totalling $1,000 per month, was adequate for his $3,500 monthly expenses. Unfortunately, his savings were invested in GICs and they all matured in 1996; the best five-year rate available for reinvestment then was 5%. This cut his investment income down to $20,000 annually, a drop of $16,000—leaving not enough to cover his expenses.

At that point Harry and his 55-year-old son, Jack, and 53-year-old daughter, Susan, decided to consider alternatives. They brought our office in to help.

One problem to overcome was that 100% of the GIC investments were with one major bank. This significantly exceeded the $60,000 Canadian Deposit Insurance Corporation (CDIC) limit per institution. The balance was un-protected. Moving some of the GICs to other institutions easily solved that.

Jack and Susan encouraged Harry to consider some growth investments. For several years they each had owned some good-quality mutual funds with annual growth rates in the 10% to 12% range.

We met with the family and presented a plan involving a shift in asset mix to 50/50 fixed income and modest growth investments. The $200,000 would go into GICs at 5% for five years. For the remaining $200,000 we recommended good-quality, balanced mutual funds. On top of that we suggested that 10% of the mutual funds be placed in a yearly systematic withdrawal program (SWP). The goal was twofold; they wanted to generate:

◆ $10,000 from interest income
◆ $20,000 from the SWP program

for a total of $30,000 yearly.

The $30,000 together with Harry's pension and OAS would cover the $3,500 monthly retirement-home costs. We made sure the family understood that there was always some volatility inherent in mutual funds. We also showed them that the long-term growth rates on equity funds averaged approximately 11% per year over time, and we demonstrated that the capital would remain intact during the next five-year period if the fund achieved this return, despite withdrawing $20,000 each year.

We also described to them the quality of the companies held by the equity portion of the mutual fund (mainly blue chip Canadian and international) along with good-quality federal and provincial bonds. The family felt comfortable with this.

In early 1997 we implemented the plan. In 18 months the growth SWP program has generated an annualized rate of return of 12%. The client has taken $30,000 out of the plan during that period, yet the capital has grown by $6,000 to $206,000.

A SWP is a service offered by most mutual fund companies. It is flexible and provides investors with needed income from unregistered investment savings. You withdraw money at regular intervals—usually monthly, quarterly or yearly—by redeeming mutual fund units (this is done by the company for you). The balance continues to be invested in well-managed equity, balanced or bond mutual funds. The SWP also allows the investor to redeem enough units to provide income that is indexed to inflation for a significantly longer period of time than if they had only invested in a GIC-type investment.

One big advantage of an SWP program is that you receive favourable tax treatment of money you withdraw. This is because only the capital gains portion of each withdrawal is taxable; the remaining portion is considered a return of the investor's original capital and is not taxable. In the early years, SWP withdrawals are primarily a return of capital and so taxes due are minimized. As time progresses, a larger portion of withdrawals will be in the form of capital gains and thus subject to tax, although unlike interest income, only 75% of capital gains are taxable.

SYSTEMATIC WITHDRAWAL

Fund purchase price	$100,000
Monthly withdrawal	$825
At end of five years:	
Total income withdrawn	51,975
Remaining fund value	138,692
At end of 10 years:	
Total income withdrawn	101,475
Remaining fund value	160,856
At the end of 1996:	
Total income withdrawn	150,975
Remaining fund value	263,464
Amount available for estate, increased:	
At end of five years, by	$38,692
At end of 10 years, by	$60,856
At the end of 1996, by	$163,464

This example (different from the one described in the text) is based on the actual performance of a conservative, Canadian equity mutual fund, starting in September, 1981. Dividends have been reinvested. You would have taken out a pre-tax annual income of $9,900 (about 10% of the original fund amount), yet the fund value continued to increase substantially.
Source: The Money Gap

Have your cake and eat it, too

Over the long-term all these factors mean that a minimum, if any, of an investor's savings are likely to be depleted. The original capital is maintained, however, only if the income withdrawn is no more or less than the growth of the mutual fund.

SWPs generally are a better bet than the Canada Savings Bonds (CSBs) used by so many people to fund retirement income. The following table shows why. Starting with the same amount, $100,000, the SWP not only delivers more after-tax monthly income, but its original investment has grown substantially even after many years of withdrawals. The original CSB investment remains at $100,000.

INCOME: MUTUAL FUND VS. CANADA SAVINGS BONDS

Date	Fund value	Annual cash with-drawal	After-tax fund income	CSB value	Annual CSB income	After-tax CSB income
1/9/81	$96,000	0		$100,000	0	
31/12/81	94,356	2,475	2,475	$100,000	3,602	2,161
12/82	94,718	9,900	9,541	$100,000	19,500	11,700
12/83	123,055	9,900	8,292	$100,000	12,000	7,200
12/84	117,213	9,900	8,861	$100,000	9,660	5,796
12/85	141,359	9,900	9.386	$100,000	11,250	6,750
12/86	138,692	9,900	9,263	$100,000	9,000	5,400
12/87	138,621	9,900	9,268	$100,000	7,861	4,717
12/88	154,384	9,900	8,344	$100,000	9,000	5,400
12/89	172,794	9,900	8,373	$100,000	10,160	6,096
12/90	142,508	9,900	8,543	$100,000	10,910	6,546
12/91	160,856	9,900	9,257	$100,000	10,750	6,450
12/92	161,296	9,900	9,598	$100,000	7,500	4,500
12/93	210,500	9,900	9,746	$100,000	6,000	3,600
12/94	205,810	9,900	8,293	$100,000	5,125	3,075
12/95	218,188	9,900	4,072	$100,000	6,375	3,825
31/12/96	263,464	9,900	6,606	$100,000	6,750	4,050
TOTAL:	**$263,464**		**$129,916**	**$100,000**		**$87,266**

This example is based on the same conservative, Canadian equity mutual fund as in the previous illustration, and assumes an income tax rate of 40%. During the 15 years, you would have enjoyed a cumulative income of $129,916. At the same time, your mutual fund would have grown by 163%. If you had chosen a more aggressive fund, you could have gained much more in fund value: to $594,553.
Source: The Money Gap

Get more than it seems from mortgage-backed securities

Harry and Maude were other, soon-to-be clients of mine and they were getting worried. Because interest rates had dropped so low, their retirement income had slid to a point slightly below what they needed to maintain a comfortable life style. In their late 60s, they had the usual private pension, CPP and OAS income, but they depended on a little extra income from savings to allow them a comfortable, though still modest, lifestyle. They were beginning to wonder whether they would have to sell their small bungalow to give them the extra money they needed each month.

They had read about reverse mortgages providing income to mature retirees, so they thought they might investigate. Neighbours had mentioned our office as a source of reliable information, so one day Harry and Maude made an appointment.

After examining their current financial situation (modest), and their tolerance for risk (low), we agreed that in the context of their financial plan they might look into mortgage-backed securities (MBSs) rather than a reverse mortgage. MBSs are great for maximizing income within a guaranteed investment. They're ideal for retired people on fixed incomes, who want security but at the same time a reasonably high rate of return.

Most of Harry and Maude's savings were in GICs and term deposits, with an unusually high amount in bank accounts earning practically nothing. We suggested they take their bank cash and some term deposits that were shortly due to mature, and buy an MBS for $100,000. This would generate a little bit more than enough to make up for their shrinking interest-based income.

An MBS is a government-guaranteed (with some limitations) package of mortgages. Harry and Maude bought one for $100,000 at 9% (this example is based on rates prevalent a few years ago). They would receive

MORTGAGE-BACKED SECURITY

Year	Total Income	Interest Portion	Capital Portion
1	$10,076	$8,904	$1,172
2	20,072	17,696	2,376
3	30,072	26,376	3,696
4	39,236	34,216	5,020
5	49,232	42,632	6,600
Total	49,232	42,632	6,600

Harry and Maude bought a 9% MBS for $100,000. After five years they would have received $42,632 in interest payments, and $6,600 return of capital. The balance of the mortgage would be $93,400. Add that to the $6,600 and they would still have their original $100,000 to reinvest.
Source: The Money Gap

about $10,076 income every year (or approximately $839.66 per month) for five years. This seems to be a return of more than 9%, but remember that part of the payment is a return of principal, which is not taxable. The previous MBS table shows the yearly interest-income portion they will get, the return-of-capital-portion and cumulative totals.

An MBS usually carries a five-year term. Harry and Maude would be wise not to spend the entire payout each year. If they set aside the returned-principal portion in a savings account, and in five years add it to the $93,400 principal they get back from the MBS, they'll have their original $100,000 to reinvest. In the meantime they will have enjoyed a better-than-average return.

A mature investor has various ways to maximize income

Seniors, unless they have more money than they need, require an increase in their capital asset base to keep pace with the real rate of inflation if they want to maintain their standard of living. There are a number of ways to do this, apart from what I have just described.

The first move to make is to become involved in post-retirement planning. Your personal financial planning process should not end with retirement. Attend seminars that examine alternative financial techniques and products. Relearn how to restructure your financial world and consider it a continuous process. Nothing remains static, and that includes your state of health, your expectations, income needs, taxation and the effect of taxation on your standard of living.

Here are a few other income-maximizing techniques to consider:

♦   Learn how to manage low interest rates in conjunction with the rate of inflation. Rates themselves are not necessarily a bad thing.

♦   If you do use GICs, in whole or in part, to fund retirement income, learn how to stagger their maturities to gain the best return.

♦   Don't discount using annuities to fund all or part of your retirement income. A prescribed annuity can bring you more income than you might expect, and at a lower rate of tax.

♦   If you have enough retirement income for the foreseeable future, a back-to-back annuity can help you leave more than you might otherwise to children or other beneficiaries.

♦   When you mature your RRSP, use a registered retirement income fund (RRIF) to fund at least some of your further retirement income needs.

A second option would be to use an insured RRIF that might help you leave more to your beneficiaries.

♦ Learn to accept a little more risk in the form of equity investment to earn more retirement income. If you don't use some equities in your portfolio, it might not keep pace with inflation, not to mention exceed it. Don't forget, equities outperform other investments in any five-year period 72% of the time; in any 20-year period, 93% of the time.

♦ Consider a reverse mortgage. Use the equity in your home to obtain more retirement income. Reverse mortgages are not yet available in all parts of Canada. But their availability, and use, is growing. They are useful in specific circumstances; talk to a professional financial planner who knows about their ins and outs of reverse mortgages before taking the plunge.

♦ For that matter, if you want or need to embellish your income later in life, a well-qualified financial planner can almost always help. When you are sick, you seek help from a doctor; if your income is ailing, seek out an expert financial planner.

STEPHEN DEFALCO is a qualified professional planner in Ottawa with a background of more than 25 years in the banking and trust company fields and close to 30 years in the financial services industry.

He chose to work with Money Concepts because it provides the strength of a national organization combined with the independence of access to a broad range of products and services from many different financial institutions, which he may use to implement clients' personal financial plans.

Stephen is from Ottawa and is married to Patricia. They have two children. When he is not busy with his business, he enjoys golf, skiing, cycling, travel and reading. He is currently the director of the Make-A-Wish Foundation, and has been involved with the Boy Scouts, the Board of Trade and the Lung Association.

Steve may be reached by telephone at 613-721-8588 and by fax at 613-721-9456.

3

How to Accumulate Wealth

*It's not how much you save
But what you do with what you save*   By Chris Gordon

*W*e live in a materialistic society and that is not so bad. Materialism leaves us in more comfort and convenience than our forbears could imagine. It also provides opportunities for almost everybody to share in the good life.

To a large extent our good fortune has been handed to us without great effort on our part: first by a generous (some say over-generous) social safety net; second by a demographic baby-boom population bulge that helped drive up real estate values and the stock market. This added enormously to the net worth of baby-boom parents.

But the trend today is towards financial responsibility, which has led to a careful appraisal and in some cases a retrenchment of the social safety net. We now live in a social climate that demands more self-reliance. Unless we take our financial futures in our own hands, many of us who expect to be among the "Haves" in society will become the "Have-Nots."

As I drive swiftly along the highway from farm to town, I sometimes think back to my grandparents who spent their early years riding around in a horse and buggy, living in a two-room cabin and literally cutting their farms out of the forest. Just two generations later, I live in superlative comfort in an air-conditioned, four-bedroom house equipped with a dishwasher, microwave oven, a large refrigerator that spews forth ice cubes on demand, watching a television hooked into a satellite system that can pick up hundreds of stations from around the world.

When my grandparents travelled this route from farm to store about once a month, they would make the five-mile winter trip in a horse-drawn cutter. They had to heat stones and bricks and pile them at their feet, then bury themselves in blankets and hope they wouldn't become frostbitten during the two-hour journey. Today I think nothing of jumping into either of my two climate-controlled vehicles with state-of-the-art sound systems to make the same journey in about five minutes—several times a day, if I need to.

If I need one of the cars repaired, it usually takes a lot less time than it took my grandfather to nurse a horse back to health. His economic survival depended on the health of the horses. Now my family and I keep horses for recreational riding on the old homestead.

Life is a great deal different from my grandparents' days and it continues to change and evolve. Whether we like it or not, our world is moving towards a two-class society of Haves and Have-Nots. The sooner we realize this, the sooner we can take steps to ensure that we will be among the Haves. Mind you, even today's Have-Nots are a lot better off than the Have-Nots of two or more generations ago. But not well enough off, and they will slide steadily backwards towards financial frostbite unless they start quickly to pull up their socks. If Have-nots expect anything much beyond the very basic necessities in life in the future, they had better start cthinking now about accumulating wealth.

Wealth will be a necessity, not a luxury

If you are a baby boomer, like myself, wealth later in life will not be so much a luxury as a necessity. By the time my generation retires, the government-will-look-after-me mentality will be a thing of the past, like my grandparents' horse and cutter. Government coffers will simply not be full enough to provide a decent retirement income for every one of us. That's not the scariest part. We are living considerably longer than the generations preceding us. As we get older, our bodies require more attention and tend to break down more than they did in younger years. Who do you think will pick up the tab for our healthcare? Only the wealthy will be able to pay for the best available health services. The poor, on the other hand, will have no choice but to participate in what is left of a mediocre, publicly funded health system and keep their fingers crossed as they line up to receive their share of care. The healthcare consideration alone motivates me personally to continue with an aggressive wealth-accumulation program.

There are other reasons to accumulate a decent retirement fund. Money may not be able to buy happiness; true happiness after all is an inward matter that involves non-material attitudes surrounding family, friends and spirituality. But reasonable financial strength is an important factor in maintaining a reasonable quality of life. As a friend of mine says, "Anybody who says money can't buy happiness just doesn't know where to shop."

I deal with many retirees, some very wealthy and some not so wealthy, and they all have their individual definitions of the good life. Most like to drive new cars instead of living with the added stress that a clunker could leave them stranded on an unfamiliar roadside. Travel is important to many of them and they enjoy the freedom of being able to take a cruise or go on a European holiday without always worrying whether they can afford it. Many clients experience the joy and satisfaction of helping grandchildren with college or university funding. Some like to be able to help their children with a down payment for a new home. None of this would be possible if they had not made wealth accumulation a priority over the years.

Can anyone learn to accumulate wealth?

As a financial planner for many years, I have heard every excuse in the book why people can't save money. It is simply never convenient to start saving. Grant Sylvester put it wonderfully in his bestselling book on financial planning, *The Money Jar*:

> *Every one of you reading these words (and I am no exception) could provide a list as long as your arm why you can't cut back and start saving the minute you put down this book. If it is January, obviously you can't start now because you are still paying off the Christmas bills. February is just as bad because you are still getting over Christmas bills and trying to put a little aside for theater tickets and a couple of dinners out. You'd really like to join friends for a week's skiing at Whistler or the Laurentians. By March you are feeling the full effects of winter's expenses: heating costs, a new winter coat, winter tires for the car, etc. In April it is out of the question because you've got to pay the balance of income tax due. May and June are inconvenient because you have to spend a fair amount on annuals and fertilizer for the garden or spruce up your home with a paint job and get ready for summer vacation. In July and August you are spending everything you have on a well-earned vacation. Vacations are over by September but the kids are back in school and university and they need new clothes, textbooks, travel and tuition*

fees. October is a bad month for saving. You may be helping the children with travel costs when they come home for Thanksgiving or replacing aging living room furniture. In November you start the Christmas-shopping process, and naturally it's out of the question to cut back in December because of the extra costs of the festive season. In fact, December often eats up not only any surplus you have laboriously built up but frequently dumps you into a financial pit from which you have to start climbing in January. The cycle repeats itself each year, and each year you're becoming more entrenched.

So what's the answer? There is never a convenient time to start saving, so the only time is right now. You have to start saving today, systematically and with regularity. There will never be a time in life when it is easier. You know the story: when you are young, you're enjoying yourself, you are trying to make up for the bare (financial) subsistence of school days. You want to buy a car, do some traveling— all those things that are important to do before you settle down and get married. Ask a 20-year-old if it's a convenient time to save. Nine-and-a-half times out of ten you'll get the answer: "Certainly not. The idea is ridiculous."

A 30-year-old will tell you that the cost of establishing a home, perhaps marrying and starting to raise a family, precludes any type of savings. A 40-year-old will advise you that the cost of education or moving to a larger home is so overwhelming that it's an impossible time to save. Most 50-year-olds will agree that it's getting too late for serious saving and they wish they had started in their 20s or 30s. To start in your 50s you have to think in terms of saving 20% to 40% of your income if you want a reasonable retirement standard of living. And that's really tough.

Despite such excuses, I am totally convinced that anyone, regardless of age or income, can systematically save money. If they don't it's because they live by the formula, **I–E=S** (income minus expenses equals savings). This formula almost guarantees that you will never have any money left to save.

Possibly you could tinker with the formula and increase the income part of the equation by getting a second job or a better-paying job. The problem is that most of the time expenses will always rise to match income.

The only way to establish an effective savings program is to totally change the formula to **I−S=E** (income minus savings equals expenses). Another way of putting this simply is, *Pay yourself first.*

This concept goes back to Babylonian days. As Grant Sylvester wrote, "You pay yourself first—and I mean first—before you pay anything to anyone else, including your rent and your taxes."

It always amazes me that when most people collect their pay, the first thing they do is take a chunk of it and give it to the bank for their mortgage payment. Then they take another bundle and give it to the grocery store for food. Another lump goes to the restuarant for coffee and so on and so on. When they finish distributing their cash around there never seems to be anything left to save.

If these individuals just took their savings right off the top of their cheques—first thing—they'd find that they would still be able to pay their bills and their standard of living would not drop much.

If we look analytically at spending habits, we find that expenses occur in two categories:

1.   discretionary
2.   non-discretionary

Discretionary expenses are entertainment, clothing, gifts, etc. They change from month to month and the amounts are not fixed in stone. Non-discretionary are fixed costs like mortgage and car payments, monthly utility bills and other predetermined monthly commitments. Discretionary spending is what does in so many people because they can keep spending until their money is all gone. If you were to establish a monthly savings plan and pay yourself *first*, retirement saving becomes non-discretionary like your mortgage. Sure, the amount available for discretionary spending shrinks but provided the amount you pay yourself first is reasonable, you will find your standard of living will not change radically.

It took me four years in the planning business before I realized that this principle could revolutionize my financial life. I started using it myself and have never stopped. Since then I have witnessed countless people with modest or even quite low incomes become financially solid within 10 years because they adopted the principle. I have seen many others with much higher incomes still struggling financially after 10 years because they did not pay themselves first.

Don't overdo it

It is important to be reasonable when you pay yourself first. For example, if your monthly take-home pay is $2,500 and you decide that you want to pay yourself $500, you will probably fall flat on you face. As a general rule I recommend that clients pay themselves between 5% and 15% of their monthly take-home pay. If you don't earn a lot, allocate about 5%. As your income grows, increase your own pay proportionally, possibly to 15% or even higher depending on your commitment. In real money, a person earning $2,500 per month should be able to afford to set aside $125. If you make $5,000 per month, earmark about $500 for savings.

How the government will help you

Once you have made the commitment, the government will help you ease the strain of saving or will maximize the amount that you do save. You can receive a tax deduction simply by making a contribution to a registered retirement savings plan (RRSP) . Depending on your income and tax bracket, the government will reduce your tax bill by up to half of what you contribute. If you are in the top tax bracket, for every dollar you invest in an RRSP you will recover about half. Most middle-income Canadians with a taxable annual income of approximately $40,000 could save about 40% of their RRSP contributions at tax time.

This benefit is simply too huge to overlook. Yet studies show that the majority of Canadians still don't take advantage of this simple but powerful wealth-building technique. Those who do, enjoy a sizeable tax refund every spring. They may reinvest this into their RRSP or use it to reduce their debts (and interest costs). Or they might simply spend it in good conscience knowing that their long-term savings goals are well in hand.

Why wait? Get it now

Not only do you pay less tax when you contribute to an RRSP, if you play your cards right, you can pay less right away and increase your take-home pay. I should say forms, perhaps, not cards—if you are employed and receive regular income, you may file a source-deduction form with Revenue Canada. It advises the government about your regular RRSP contributions so Revenue Canada may then authorize your employer's payroll department to deduct less tax each month at source. If, for instance, you contribute $200 a month to your RRSP and you are in a 40% tax bracket, you would immediately see an $80 pay increase each month. It's a way of getting your tax refund immediately instead of waiting until the following spring.

The real benefit of an RRSP is not, however, a yearly tax reduction or an increase in take-home pay. An RRSP allows you to shelter savings from tax over the years so the magic of time and compounding growth will allow you to pull a genuine and notable retirement fund out of your savings hat. As the following table illustrates, the benefit from saving money inside a tax-sheltered investment is significantly greater than from saving outside.

TOTAL SAVED AFTER:

	10 YEARS	15 YEARS	20 YEARS	30 YEARS	40 YEARS
Outside RRSP:	$22,407	$42,512	$72,603	$185,055	***$436,973***
Inside RRSP:	39,309	83,507	161,397	540,585	***1,718,285***

These figures are based on a modest contribution of $1,400 net each year, earning 12% interest, and subject to a 30% tax rate (for non-RRSP savings).
Source: The Money Gap

Clients frequently ask me, "What kind of RRSP should I buy?" I usually answer that there are a myriad of choices from many institutions but it boils down to choosing among three types of RRSPs: a poor RRSP; a good RRSP and a great RRSP. Here is why I name them that way:

The poor RRSP

Mr. and Mrs. Brown, both age 30, contribute a total of $2,500 annually to an RRSP. They are busy people and don't want to be bothered periodically with major investment decisions. Their main reason for contributing is the tax refund they'll get. So they open a savings-account RRSP at their bank. The money is not locked up for a specific period of time as with GICs, but it earns interest at a rate of about 1% per year. If the Browns were to faithfully contribute their $2,500 annually until they retire at age 65, (and if rates stayed the same) they would have $108,733.70 in their RRSP. This may seem like a lot of money but I would call it a pretty poor RRSP.

A good RRSP

The Browns' neighbours, the Smiths, are also age 30 and they also work for the same employer. They too have decided to make a $2,500-per-year RRSP contribution. Like the Browns they look forward to a tax break each spring, but they've done enough research and reading to conclude that the Browns' savings-account RRSP probably isn't the wisest choice. They opt for what I would call a good RRSP—each year they buy a five-year, $2,500 guaranteed investment certificate (GIC) as their contribution. During the next 35 years the Smiths might average not a 1% but a 5% yield on their money (assuming rates stay the same). At 65, the Smiths would retire and be pleasantly surprised to discover that their RRSPs had grown to $250,880.85. That's more than twice the amount the Browns would have. Over the years the Smiths would contribute exactly the same amount of money as the Browns and enjoy the same standard of living. This is what I call a good RRSP.

A great RRSP

Right across the street from the Browns and Smiths live the Bests. They too felt that contributing $2,500 each year to an RRSP was about all they could afford. Unlike their neighbours who went to the bank for their RRSP, the Bests decided to seek the advice of a professional financial planner. Their planner spent a lot of time gathering information about their financial situation, assessed their risk preference and helped them define and clarify their long- and short-term goals. After a couple of meetings, their advisor presented the Bests with a written financial plan that was to become their road map to success. It laid out everything in black and white, from where they were to begin, to where they wanted to be, financially, at retirement and how to get there. As part of their financial plan, the Bests decided on what I consider a great RRSP.

The great RRSP starts with the advice and direction of a qualified financial advisor. In the Bests' case, their advisor suggested using equity mutual funds initially within an RRSP. Over the years the plan would call for spreading the risk by diversifying into a number of funds. They would use various wealth-building strategies, such as using the maximum foreign content and diversifying among various management styles.

The Bests would meet with their financial advisor once or twice per year to assess their investments and make sure that their financial plan was on track. There would be years when the Bests' investments would seem to leapfrog ahead and other years where their balance actually would drop from the previous year. There would also be times when the advisor would suggest switching some of the funds to others because of disappointing performances.

Following this plan, the Bests remained faithful to their commitment of contributing $2,500 annually and maintaining a long-term investment perspective. As a result, they would be able to average a 12% rate of return over the 35 years. When they retire, they would discover to their delight that their RRSP balance was $1,340,656.84. That's what I call a great RRSP.

To sum up I would like to add to the precepts of paying yourself first, and using tax-sheltered investments (mainly RRSPs) to build wealth, my personal four basic principles for investment success:

PRINCIPLE ONE: USE PROFESSIONALS

There has been so much written about financial planning during the past few years, a misconception seems to have emerged: everyone should and can become an investment whiz. This is absolutely false for two reasons. First of all, it takes more than reading a few books or magazine articles to properly understand the financial-planning process. This takes years of experience and rigorous continuing education programs. Professional planners offer this. Most do-it-yourself investors spend only enough time managing their investments to become dangerous and are their own worst enemy. According to a survey conducted in the United States by Dalbor Inc., covering a 12-year period, there was a significant difference in results between investors with advisors and those without. Advisor-assisted investors outperformed self-directed investors by more than 16% during that time.

Secondly, many people are not truly interested in the esoterics of investing. They are busy managing their own careers and do not have either the interest or the time to research, read, trade and worry about investments. That's where a professional financial advisor comes in. This does not mean that investors should take a totally hands-off approach—they should meet regularly with their advisor and over time develop a comfortable and professional relationship. The result of professional help is peace of mind, which you can't buy at the supermarket, along with the bonus of spending more spare time enjoying yourself.

PRINCIPLE TWO: USE TAX-EFFICIENT STRATEGIES

The most obvious strategy is to take full advantage of the RRSP system—it provides both short- and long-term financial benefits. You get immediate tax relief as well as long-term tax deferral on the growth of contributions within the plan.

Another strategy—outside RRSP savings—is to take full advantage of the relatively low capital gains tax rate. For example, if you buy stock for $10,000 and sell it for $20,000 five years later, your capital gain is $10,000. The tax liability is 75% of the capital gain at your marginal tax rate. If you had earned the same amount in the form of interest, you would pay more in tax.

PRINCIPLE THREE: INVEST IN EQUITIES WHEN YOU CAN

When you buy equity mutual funds or a common stock, you are actually buying ownership in a business or businesses. When you buy a GIC you are actually lending money to an institution. History has proven again and again that over time you will do much better owning a piece of a well-managed business than by lending your money to an institution at current interest rates, especially today's rates. Other chapters in this book deal with that subject in more depth. Read them and profit from the advice.

PRINCIPLE FOUR: INVEST FOR THE LONG TERM

One of the greatest investors of our time is American Warren Buffet. He uses two principles when investing:

1. Invest in great businesses that are well managed.

2. Hold these investments for the long term.

Buffet has amassed a fortune with that approach. Unfortunately, our society tends to think short term. The various media frequently encourage the investing public to anticipate what the best investment will be for the next six months. This is called market timing and timers hope to capitalize on short-term investments and then move on to the next red-hot opportunity.

Buffet and others are evidence that this method seldom works. Invest in quality and leave it alone for at least 10 years. This approach has the added benefit of avoiding the emotional swings accompanying short-term market fluctuation. Historically, the long-term, patient investor in quality is always rewarded.

We live in a wonderful world filled with a great deal of opportunity and choice. If we are going to live here anyway, it can be a lot more comfortable if we have wealth on our side. Remember, the choice is ours.

CHRIS GORDON is president of Money Concepts in Sault Ste. Marie, Ontario. As a professional financial planner, he believes one of his main objectives in business is to eliminate the confusion and stress clients often associate with managing their financial affairs. That is why he and his team emphasize integrity, professionalism and trust when developing long-term relationships with clients.

Chris and his colleagues offer the full gamut of comprehensive financial planning services including estate, retirement and investment planning, as well as access to a full range of financial products, such as mutual funds, RRSPs and life and disability insurance.

One of the most gratifying aspects of his business life is that, while achieving his own financial goals, Chris is helping clients attain theirs at the same time.

Chris, his wife, Kathy, and their three children live on and operate a small hobby farm where their favourite activity is caring for and riding horses. They also enjoy travelling.

Chris may be reached by telephone at 705-942-6113 and by fax at 705-942-6114.

4

If You Don't Know Where You're Going, You're Not Likely to Get There

A personal view of financial planning By Rob Hodgkinson
CFP

*W*ayne slumped back in his chair obviously frustrated, and looked at the neat stacks of paper bisecting the family room floor with precision. In front of him the computer screen saver flashed and hungry caterpillars marched across the monitor, munching on green pixels.

"What's the matter, hon?" Wayne's wife, Jen, laid a sympathetic hand on his shoulder as she surveyed the room.

"Do you realize," he said, "that I could recite to you our yearly household heating costs for the past seven years? And I have all the paperwork from our conversion to natural gas, even the cost of oil for the five years before that?"

Jen shrugged. "That's great. I always appreciate how organized you are."

"That's just it!" Wayne's voice betrayed his exasperation. "I'm organized alright. I know where we've spent our money and I've got the receipts to prove it. But I feel we have no control over our finances or what's in store for us financially. Last year, for instance, I bought an RRSP at the bank, but I have no idea if it's the best one for us or what it will do for us down the road. I'm not sure what to do at this point."

"Wayne, remember that sign downtown that has changing messages on it? I think it's from a financial planning centre. When I drove past yesterday it said, *Wisdom Gives Wings to Knowledge*. It kind of stuck in my mind, but maybe some of that kind of wisdom is what we need. With your facts and a professional's financial wisdom, maybe it will come together."

"Jen, that's worth thinking about." Wayne grabbed a brochure off one of the neat paper stacks as the caterpillars continued to munch across the screen. He seemed to have regained his natural optimism. "This one is from the Canadian Association of Financial Planners and it says that a financial planner is a person who, number one, clarifies your present financial situation; number two, identifies financial goals and objectives; and number three, identifies financial problems and opportunities. Wow! We have a murky financial situation and I don't think we've ever talked about our goals and objectives. Or what financial problems or opportunities we might run into down the line, for that matter.

"Listen, there's more. A planner should, number four, provide written recommendations and alternative solutions; number five, coordinate the implementation of the recommendations; and number six, provide periodic reviews and updates.

"Jen, what do you think? Our record keeping is good. We know how much money we have in the bank and what bills need to be paid. But we really don't know whether we're further ahead today than we were five years ago. And I don't know whether things will be any better five years from now. And what about retirement? I assume we'll be able to retire before we reach 65, but I don't have the faintest idea how we'll be able to finance that. Maybe a financial planner is our missing link and can help bring it all together."

A week later but light years ahead

Jen and Wayne shared the loveseat in front of the fireplace in the family room, sipping hot chocolate. They often spent evenings there enjoying the comfortable warmth. Before they got too relaxed, Wayne reached for the clipboard on the floor beside him.

"Well, what's your opinion?" he asked. "What do you think about the meeting this morning?" They had spent the past several evenings discussing their financial situation and what sort of direction they might take. That morning, they took the plunge and met with a local financial planner who had advised one of Wayne's co-workers.

"I was impressed, Wayne. I didn't know what to expect, but I felt very comfortable with Bill. Partly because of his experience, I guess; but he seemed to understand our concerns and our dreams. And he certainly seemed to know a lot about investments and life insurance. I think we could trust him to guide us in the right financial direction. What he said about balancing living for today with planning effectively for tomorrow especially appealed to me."

"I felt the same way," Wayne replied. "It was almost like chatting with a friend. It didn't take me long to realize that even if I had the time, I don't have the expertise to sift through all that information on mutual funds and RRSPs and insurance and investment options."

"You're right," said Jen. "I also liked the fact that he is an independent planner and not tied to any particular alternative. He could create a plan for us and recommend the best investment options just for us from a huge number of financial product suppliers out there. And I like knowing that he would continue working with us every year to help keep our plan on track and accountable.

"Wayne, remember Lisa from the health club? She and her husband bought some financial-planning software and I remember her telling me how much time they spent gathering information, keying in data and running all sorts of "what if" scenarios. I ran into her yesterday and asked how it was going. Would you believe they haven't done anything? All that work, but they just couldn't decide what was best for them, so nothing happened."

Wayne shook his head. "That's a shame. I've become a believer in expertise. As Bill said, everyone relies on their doctor or mechanic or lawyer for their wisdom. It's the same with a financial planner—the right planner, anyway. It could mean the difference between assembling or foregoing thousands of dollars over our lifetime. So it's a go as far as you are concerned? We'll meet Bill again next week and get started."

If you don't know where you're going, you're not likely to get there

---

Jen waited, sipping her decaffeinated coffee and watching the door. Since the couple were both working late that evening, they had agreed to meet at a neighbourhood 1950s-type restaurant for a quick meal on the way home. Jen waved as Wayne came in. Within minutes, the waitress had poured more coffee, taken their orders and returned with their dinners.

Jen was the first to mention their meeting with Bill. "How did you feel about our information-gathering session this morning?"

"When Bill said it would be a time to gather information, I was expecting hard facts and figures, like take-home pay, the value of our house and outstanding debts," Wayne said. "I'm glad I could answer those questions, but I have to admit I was surprised by some of the soft information that he wanted. I've never really thought about what I wanted to do at retirement. Or what I expected of retirement, either. It's always been a sort of future, hazy don't-set-an-alarm-clock kind of thing in the back of my mind."

Jen stole a french fry from Wayne's plate. "I didn't expect his questions about our children and parents. You and I have talked generally about the costs of educating the kids, but I had never thought about whether we should consider planning an inheritance for them as an important feature of our lives. I guess it does make sense for him to ask about our parents. It would certainly affect our plans and our lives if we had to be financially responsible for your parents or my mother."

"Or if we are likely to receive a huge inheritance."

Jen ignored the interruption. "We should be thankful that they can care for themselves. But I do wonder whether their wills are current. And I don't remember either your parents or Mom ever discussing a power of attorney for health or property. Gee, Wayne, now that I think about it, a couple of years ago Mom and I talked briefly about the insurance money she got when Dad died. She said that she was just going to leave it in her chequing account in case she needed it. I bet it's still there, not earning a penny of interest. I'll have to talk to her about that. Perhaps she should talk to Bill, too."

Wayne drained his coffee cup. "Well, Bill obviously has us thinking. It's going to be interesting to see how he pulls all of this stuff together."

Jen slid out of the booth. "Wayne, did you notice the sign?"

"What sign?"

"The one at Bill's office. On the side of the building. It said, If you don't know where you're going, you're not likely to get there. After this morning, I think we have a better idea where we are going. I really look forward to seeing the plan Bill puts together."

Another week later they know where they are going —and how to get there

---

Jen was already settled on the loveseat, casually leafing through their copy of the financial plan prepared by Bill. "Wayne, remember that CAFP brochure we looked at a couple of weeks ago? It mentioned that a financial planner is someone who clarifies your present situation. Do you think Bill did that this morning when he went over the plan?"

"No question in my mind," Wayne said. Bill had certainly clarified their current situation. Neatly detailed in the plan was their Net Worth Statement. Based on Wayne's records and their conversation, Bill had produced a snapshot of where they were, financially. As he said, this was a benchmark so they could check on progress from this point. The Net Worth Statement presented a neat computer printout of their assets, divided into cash, investments, real estate and personal property. It also provided a recap of both their long-term and short-term debt.

"Wayne, did you have any idea that we were worth as much as we are?"

Wayne couldn't conceal his pleasure. "Wasn't that great? And a clarification of how much insurance we have and what my pension plan will be worth. I was also surprised at your RRSP eligibility amount."

"He certainly helped us identify our financial goals and objectives," Jen said. "I found it helpful to set out how much cash we felt we might need in case of an emergency. And to talk about why one buys life insurance and how much and what type. I always thought that insurance was something that you bought when you were young, and paid for until you retired. Then you had it until you died. It never occurred to me to calculate how much life insurance coverage we would need to replace either of our incomes if one of us died while the kids are still dependants. Or that we obviously need more coverage now than we will when we have more saved for retirement in a few years.

"Then that business of planning insurance in conjunction with your pension as well as possibly putting something in place to pay taxes on our estate, if we feel that is important. That wouldn't have occurred to us at all without Bill's prompting. I certainly see now why life insurance is an important part of financial planning.

"Another thing I found helpful, " Jen continued, "was discussing how we felt about paying for the kids' education. You and I paid our own way through college, so I'd always assumed that we would help our kids out when and if we could. But with educational costs rising so much more quickly than the average cost of living *when and if* may not be enough. We may need to help more than we thought."

Retirement was just a misty idea for the future

Wayne nodded agreement. "Retirement was an area worth talking about, too. As I told you last week, I had never really seriously thought about retirement. If we implement this plan, it looks like we may be able to retire comfortably when I'm 60 with about 80% of our pre-retirement income."

Jen glanced at the CAFP brochure again. "Did he identify problems or opportunities?"

"Absolutely! The money sitting in Canada Savings Bonds is an example of an opportunity. By the time we pay tax on the interest and account for inflation, there isn't much growth left. If we move that money into an equity mutual fund registered as an RRSP, we have the potential for far greater growth. We'd get a tax rebate or deferment this year for registering the RRSP and the investment would grow in a tax-free environment as long as it stays an RRSP. So we wouldn't have to pay tax every year on CSB interest. That's an opportunity, the way I see it.

"As far as problems go, he identified our lingering balance on the department store credit card. We haven't been very smart paying more than 20% interest. We can avoid that in the future by paying off the balance and taking care of the full amount every month.

"Another opportunity," Wayne went on, "is Bill's suggestion of using mutual funds as investments. I never realized that an equity mutual fund is simply a pool of money consisting of shares of individual companies. When we buy a mutual fund, our money is diversified and spread over all the companies in that fund instead of being locked into just one or two stocks. I appreciated his explanation of the importance of choosing a well-managed fund that is attuned to our long-term objectives.

"Take a look at this." Wayne gave Jen a page with a table and chart on it. "I picked it up at Bill's office." The table demonstrated how someone investing $1 in 1956 in stocks comprising the Toronto Stock Exchange 300 Composite Stock Index, assuming all dividends were reinvested, would have had $46.80 some 42 years later in 1998. If they had invested in one particular bank's long-term bond index, they would have had just over $27. If they'd invested in three-month Treasury Bills, the result would have been about $18. If that $1 investment had grown at the rate of inflation the same time period, it would be worth around $6.

"It definitely appears that for long-term investing, equities tend to be the superior performer. There's no guarantee they'll continue to do as well, but we can't argue with the fact that stocks have outperformed other types of investments over the long haul. Since we still have a day or two until retirement, that looks like the way to go."

Living longer is expensive

Jen smiled. "I guess we are looking at the long haul. Remember, Bill pointed out that even after retiring, assuming you retire at age 60, it's still a long haul. We're going to be drawing on our retirement funds for at least 30 years, if we are lucky."

RETURN ON INVESTMENT MEANS A LOT

Years	1%	5%	8%	10%	12%
1	$10,100	$10,500	$10,800	$11,000	$11,200
2	$10,201	$11,025	$11,664	$12,100	$12,544
3	$10,303	$11,576	$12,597	$13,310	$14,049
4	$10,406	$12,155	$13,605	$14,641	$15,735
5	$10,510	$12,763	$14,693	$16,105	$17,623
6	$10,615	$13,401	$15,869	$17,716	$19,738
7	$10,721	$14,071	$17,138	$19,487	$22,107
8	$10,829	$14,775	$18,509	$21,436	$24,760
9	$10,937	$15,513	$19,990	$23,579	$27,731
10	$11,046	$16,289	$21,589	$25,937	$31,058
11	$11,157	$17,103	$23,316	$28,531	$34,785
12	$11,268	$17,959	$25,182	$31,384	$38,960
13	$11,381	$18,856	$27,196	$34,523	$43,635
14	$11,495	$19,799	$29,372	$37,975	$48,871
15	$11,610	$20,789	$31,722	$41,772	$54,736
16	$11,726	$21,829	$34,259	$45,950	$61,304
17	$11,843	$22,920	$37,000	$50,545	$68,660
18	$11,961	$24,066	$39,960	$55,599	$76,900
19	$12,081	$25,270	$43,157	$61,159	$86,128
20	$12,202	$26,533	$46,610	$67,275	$96,463
21	$12,324	$27,860	$50,338	$74,002	$108,038
22	$12,447	$29,253	$54,365	$81,403	$121,003
23	$12,572	$30,715	$58,715	$89,543	$135,523
24	$12,697	$32,251	$63,412	$98,497	$151,786
25	$12,824	$33,864	$68,485	$108,347	$170,001
Total	**$12,824**	**$33,864**	**$68,485**	**$108,347**	**$170,001**

An investment of $10,000 would grow much faster and larger if it earned an average yield of 12% rather than 1%. This example ignores the effect of taxes.

Wayne gave Jen another sheet of paper. "I printed this off earlier when I was playing with some different rates of return. If someone like your mother were to leave $10,000 in her chequing account because she thought she didn't need it, and it averaged an annual yield of 1%, at the end of 25 years she would have $12,824. If she got 5% instead, it would grow to $33,864; at 8%, it would grow to $68,485 and at 12% it would end up at $170,001.

"Jen, according to our Net Worth Statement, you have a GIC registered as an RRSP and it will mature next month at just over $10,000. It's only earning 4% now. Bill suggests you transfer it to an equity mutual fund. To my way of thinking, that is one wonderful opportunity."

"Okay, okay, point made," said Jen. "And he certainly provided a plan with written recommendations and alternative solutions."

The pay-yourself-first approach

Wayne took the financial plan from her and skimmed the Cash Flow sheet. "Jen, do you remember a couple of years ago we decided that we were going to start budgeting? We marked down every nickel that we spent, right down to a coffee at Tim Hortons. After two or three weeks, we had a humongous pile of paper and figures galore. But I didn't know what to do with it all, so we just drifted back to 'get a paycheque—pay the bills.'

"Bill's idea of *pay yourself first* makes so much more sense. We have to make the same commitment to paying ourselves as we do to paying our mortgage. If we automatically invest money into RRSPs every month, along with money for the children's education, as well as a pre-authorized amount into a money-market fund for holidays, we can spend the rest as we want without feeling like spendthrifts. I guess we always worked on the idea that income minus expenses equals savings. But there was never any money left over because expenses always seemed to grow to fit the size of our income. With Bill's method we can change the formula to read income minus savings equals expenses."

Wayne leafed through the plan. "Before we see Bill next week to start implementing the plan, we have to decide what to do about this life insurance. He's suggested three options, depending on what type of coverage we want and how much we want to spend." He skimmed further through the plan.

"This is something else that caught my attention," he mused quietly, almost to himself.

"What's that, Wayne?"

"Making interest a tax-deductible expense."

"I'm not sure I remember the details. Can you go over it again?"

Wayne slid a little closer to Jen on the loveseat so she could see the plan. "When your dad died, we didn't know what to do with the money we received, so we just bought a GIC with it, remember? Since it's maturing soon and our mortgage reopens this fall, we could apply the GIC proceeds to pay down our mortgage. Then we could borrow that same amount and use it to buy mutual funds designed for long-term growth. Our total investments remain the same and our debt has not increased, but we have effectively split the mortgage into two loans. One loan is still a mortgage on the balance we owe on the house and the other we use for investing.

"The beauty of it is that while the interest we pay on the mortgage is not tax deductible, the interest we pay on the investment loan is deductible. So we'll probably pay less tax overall."

Wayne continued to flip through the plan. He checked the educational cost calculations for the kids. "You know, I should have told Bill that Mom and Dad have mentioned a few times that they would eventually like to give some money to the kids. I'll bet Bill could suggest a way to give it to them now because I'm pretty sure there would be less tax through the years if the kids claimed it instead of Mom and Dad. Why should anybody pay more tax than needed? At the same time it's probably a good way to introduce the subject of money with Mom and Dad. Isn't it odd how hard it is sometimes to talk about money with people you are close to?"

Wills and power of attorney crucial

Jen squeezed Wayne's hand. "Be thankful that we have such an honest relationship with your parents. I think you are right; they have mentioned giving something to the kids. Let's check with Bill first to find out what options are available. When we talk with your parents about it we could bring up the subject of how current their wills are and whether they have powers of attorney in place."

Wayne tossed the plan on the end table and rubbed his eyes. "This is terrific. Bill has taken all our facts, thoughts and dreams and put them on paper. Now we have a direction we didn't before. We're lucky we found a fit with someone we trust and who understands us."

Jen watched the dancing fireplace flames. "You're right. I feel comfortable with him too, and I have confidence in his advice and experience. It's a plus that the plan is not the end of it all—we'll be working with him to implement it and we will see him from time to time to review our progress or make changes if our circumstances change."

Wayne stretched and plunked his feet onto the coffee table. "The best thing about a plan like this is the feeling we've taken more control over our life together. It would have been easy to put it off because it took some hard work, some time and a lot of thinking, which isn't always easy. But we now know where we are and where we want to go. Bill has really helped us see how we can get from here to there, and still have a life in the meantime. Jen, I guess that sign you spotted a few weeks ago was right: wisdom has given wings to knowledge."

ROB HODGKINSON is a Certified Financial Planner (CFP) and a Practitioner Member of the Canadian Association of Financial Planners. Since joining Money Concepts in 1987, he has become a partner and vice-president of the Money Concepts Financial Planning Centre in Sault Ste. Marie, Ontario. Rob has earned membership in the Money Concepts President's Club and Chairman's Club.

Rob enjoys working with clients who have a serious desire to improve their financial situation. He is experienced and able to provide strategies to allow clients to meet their goals and objectives.

Many of the clients he works with are in the mid- to upper-income range, or dual-income families. With this in mind he pays particular attention to investment strategies, tax reduction and estate and retirement planning.

Prior to his career in financial planning, Rob spent 15 years in management positions in the hospitality and transportation industries. In his leisure time, he enjoys travelling, walking and reading. He is involved with many church activities and serves as chairman of the deacon's board. He and his wife, Shelley, have two children and are long-time residents of the Sault Ste. Marie area. Rob may be reached by telephone at 705-942-6113 and by fax at 705-942-6114.

5

Create Wealth by Minimizing Tax

By Paul Jackson, BA & Craig Lehr, CFP

*I*t is often said that death and taxes are the two certainties everybody faces. Apart from being a beneficiary of medical science (and hoping for longevity genes) there is little you can do about the former. You can, however, control your tax burden to some extent—quite legally—so that you may have a financially comfortable lifestyle.

Minimizing tax—personal income tax, property tax, GST, PST and the OAS clawback—is a way of creating wealth. Every dollar you keep away from Revenue Canada is a dollar saved. You can save some of these dollars by using what we call taxation's Three Ds: Divide, Defer and Deduct. It would be prudent to use the services of a professional financial planner to invoke tax savings. In turn, your planner might well call upon the services of a lawyer and/or an accountant to ensure that the complexities of your particular financial life are dealt with in the most appropriate manner.

Here are highlights of some tax minimization strategies we employ in our practice to help lighten our clients' tax burdens:

D ONE: DIVIDE

You divide to split tax liabilities among family members. This is known as income splitting and you are simply shifting income from a family member in a higher tax bracket to another family member in a lower tax bracket. There are a number of ways to do this, but we will discuss two common methods: spousal RRSPs, and education-planning tools, such as informal in-trust accounts and Registered Education Savings Plans (RESPs). Income splitting usually does not provide immediate tax relief, but the long-term benefits can be tremendous.

Spousal RRSPs divide income to reduce tax

Let's compare the Smith and Jones families. Both families have annual gross retirement incomes of $50,000. However, Mr. Jones is the recipient of the family's pension, RRSP and CPP income. The Smiths on the other hand have split their income so that Mr. Smith receives the pension income and a 50% share of their combined CPP credits. Some 20 years previously they began a spousal RRSP for Mrs. Smith, to ensure equal incomes at retirement. Because they did this planning, they are rewarded with about $4,000 per year more in retirement than the Jones, as the diagram shows.

INCOME SPLITTING

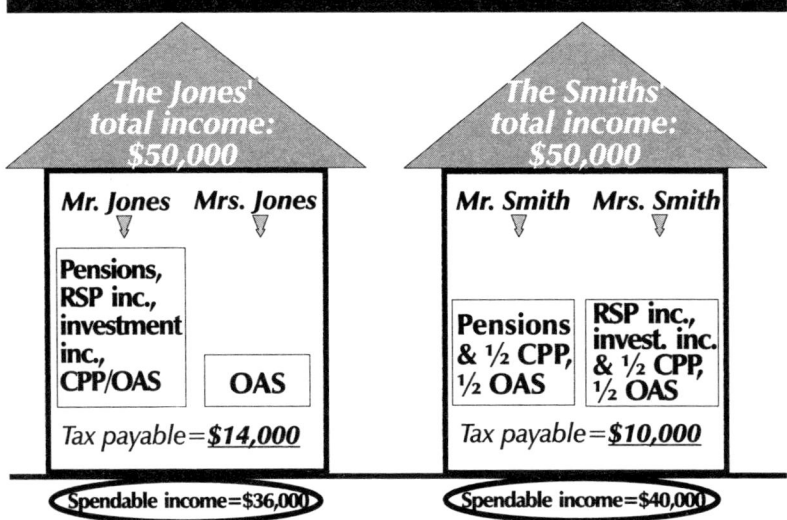

The Smiths ended up with $4,000 more per year after taxes because they wisely balanced their income between the two spouses, reducing the tax load.

Source: The Money Gap

Sometimes it is difficult to think 20 years in advance, but for maximum financial success, you should do it. This same early approach applies to planning for your children's education.

Education planning rearranges income to reduce tax

Many parents wish to assist their children with education costs, especially since post-secondary education will probably cost $100,000 per child by the year 2010. Ways to fund children's education are covered in another chapter. Our discussion about RESPs and in-trust accounts does not explain these strategies but instead points out how using such programs can minimize your personal income tax.

So, how would you like to fund these escalating education costs? If you wait until the child is in high school to decide, it is often too late: you could be forced to cash in personal investments (which incurs taxation), or fund the expense from personal cash flow. However, if you plan ahead and invest a small amount of your income in an RESP and/or in-trust account, the endeavour could be relatively painless.

Deposits you make into an RESP grow sheltered from tax ($100 per month invested for 18 years at 10% grows to $57,639). It becomes taxable when a student withdraws funds for school fees. Presumably at that point, he or she will have little or no income and thus will have to pay little or no tax. Similarly, deposits into an in-trust account will grow without tax consequence to you, provided the investments grow via capital gains. Revenue Canada's attribution rules direct capital gains (and tax liability) to the student. If the student has low or no income, tax consequences will be minimal if any. Both these strategies should be more attractive than cashing in (and paying taxes on) investments you have held for some time, to cover education costs.

D TWO: DEFER

A dollar deferred is a dollar saved. Remember that and you will save thousands of dollars on your tax bill over the years. Four tools that can enable you to defer taxes are: RRSPs, universal life insurance, tax-efficient mutual funds and the tax-efficient strategy of buying and holding.

RRSPs: the magic of tax-free compounding

Most Canadians are aware of RRSPs, though not necessarily of their full advantages. When we ask clients' opinions about RRSP benefits, most cite the yearly tax deduction resulting from a contribution. This is a benefit, all right, but hardly the most important. The significant payoff from RRSPs is the effect that years of tax-free compounding can have. Consider this comparison:3

Suppose you found an investment that paid an annual interest rate of 8%. You bought $10,000 of it every year for 25 years. Your tax bracket is 50% and the return is based only upon interest, not capital gains or dividends. At the end of 25 years you would have $433,177 after you paid taxes each year.

Place the same $10,000 investment into an RRSP tax shelter. The difference is astonishing. After the same period you would have $789,544 in the RRSP–almost double the result of the non-sheltered investment. And remember, you would have garnered an additional $125,000 or so in tax savings along the way in the form of yearly deductions. However, the tax-free compounding is the biggest benefit of all.

Universal life insurance: the newest, best-kept secret

We love to talk to clients about universal life insurance (UL) as another great tax-deferral vehicle because it surprises them. The word "insurance" often means costly premium payments to many people. To others it conjures up thoughts of mortality, and benefits that go to others only after their own death. UL is relatively new and its living benefits need some explanation. Once clients understand how it works, they become comfortable with the concept and usually begin a UL program.

You could write an entire book about the value of a well-structured UL policy, but our discussions will be limited to two strategies useful for reducing tax liability. The first–geared towards people with at least 10 years available to accumulate wealth–is called Insured Retirement. The second–Insured Inheritance–is usually a strategy for seniors.

A UL policy can provide you with a plan that will pass wealth to the next generation quickly, uncontested, tax-free, with no probate, and at the same time provide you with the living benefit of tax-sheltered investment growth. Every dollar you put into a UL policy above and beyond the minimum premium grows in an investment account completely tax sheltered, subject to a maximum set by Revenue Canada. Unlike whole-life policies, you are free to choose the investments in the sheltered account. You may choose from a broad range of investments including term deposits, equity-linked index accounts, bond indexes and regular savings accounts. You may structure it for conservative or aggressive growth, depending on your tolerance to risk and your financial goals.

Insured retirement

Imagine Jack and Mary with $10,000 per year to invest beyond their maximum annual RRSP contribution. They are both 40 years old, non-smokers, in good health (health and age matter in life insurance) and they want to retire in 20 years. For 20 years they deposit this money into a $650,000 UL policy. The minimum annual premium is $1,953, which the insurance company scoops from the investment pot. The remainder accumulates as the investment portion of the program. Jack and Mary could reasonably expect the investment pot to grow at an annual compounded rate of 8.5% for that 20-year period. The end result would be a grand total of $513,353 after two decades, including interest-rate bonuses paid by the insurance company.

If you had invested the same amount and received the same rate of return for the same length of time, but outside a tax-sheltered vehicle like the UL, you would end up with a retirement fund of only $318,614 (assuming a tax bracket of 50%). That's almost $200,000 less. It's less because you had to pay tax on the non-sheltered yield each year, and that effectively reduced the amount available to earn a return the following year. That's a pretty big price to pay compared to the $1,953 UL premium each year. Rather than going to the government, the premium gives you insurance protection along the way. For instance, if you were both to die unexpectedly in the 20th year of the policy, your heirs would receive $1,528,475 tax free.

There are more advantages—consider what happens after 20 years: Jack and Mary are retired and would like to use some of that $513,353 to supplement their pension income. They could simply make withdrawals from the policy and add the amount to their taxable income that year. However, if they want to minimize their tax liability, there is a better way (assuming they have good advice from their financial planner). They use the cash value of the policy as collateral for a series of bank loans that they spend as income with no tax liability. This allows their investment pot to continue its growth in the policy tax shelter. Most banks will lend anywhere from 50% to 90% of the policy's cash value depending on what investments it holds. This means that Jack and Mary could easily develop a tax-free income stream from this series of loans of up to $40,000 per year, and never owe the bank more than the policy amount. Also, most banks will capitalize the loans or at most demand an interest-only payment. Since the loan is fully secured, it would be paid off at the death of the last surviving policyholder (with tax-free dollars, of course).

Insured inheritance

This is an excellent strategy for people who do not need additional income and would like to pass along a sizeable amount of non-registered (non-RRSP) wealth to their children. Most people, naturally, don't want to do this until they die. Giving your money away (often termed as gifting) is a dubious strategy because you never know whether you might need it yourself. Insured inheritance allows you to have your cake and eat it, too.

Once again, assume a scenario with a couple, both 65 years old, healthy and non-smokers. They have $200,000 in term deposits earning an average rate of return of 8.5%. They don't need more income and they want the children to inherit the full amount.

What are the tax consequences of maintaining term deposits outside of a tax-sheltered vehicle? The $200,000 at 8.5% would earn $17,000 taxable interest annually, which in turn means an $8,500 tax bill (at a 50% tax bracket). What would happen if the couple paid that $8,500 instead to a life insurance company? They would be able to buy a universal policy of $660,000.

Even better would be to pass the entire $200,000 to the insurance company, attaching those funds to a UL policy. Assume the policy's investments grow at 8.5% annually. Each year a certain maximum allowable amount of the $200,000 is funnelled into the policy from a "side fund." The couple only pays taxes on the annual side-fund earnings. After about nine years the entire $200,000 will be sheltered within the policy so there is no more tax to pay. The company will take the annual policy premiums from the side fund, resulting in a self-funding program—as the owner of the policy, you should never have to pay for the premiums from your own cash flow.

Using this technique, the couple has sheltered money from tax and maintained access to the funds. By the 10th year all the money is sheltered and they have $355,698 available for their use if needed. If they have both died by the 25ᵗʰ year, their heirs would receive $1,996,788 tax free from the proceeds of the policy ($660,000 face value plus accumulated cash value). It does not take a rocket scientist to figure this is a lot better than letting the $200,000 sit in term deposits and just rolling them over at maturity.

You should only implement concepts like these under the guidance of a financial professional, knowledgeable in advanced planning strategies.

Mutual-fund investments can be tax-efficient

Mutual funds are commonplace in Canada now, so commonplace that many people invest in them without professional advice. But it's easy to make mistakes. We do not consider a short chat with a bank clerk or a discount broker sufficient if you want to obtain the best investment strategy.

Have you ever bought mutual funds outside an RRSP and received a tax slip at the end of the year advising you of capital gains, even though you had never sold even one fund unit? A professional might have advised you of the available funds that would not send you these unwanted slips that cost you needless tax. Mutual fund companies send out these tax slips because, during the course of their yearly business, they buy and sell stocks and incur capital gains. These gains flow through to unit-holders such as yourself. If the fund company bought XYZ stock five years ago at $20 per share, and sold it this year for $60, there would be a $40 per share capital gain. As an investor, how can you avoid these unwanted, taxable distributions?

One way to do that is to own funds that employ a buy-and-hold strategy. The managers of these funds are not constantly buying and selling to produce profits. Their main approach is to seek out what they believe to be quality investments and hold them for the long term. Such a fund would be tax efficient.

Consider a hypothetical example: make a $10,000 mutual-fund investment that gives you a 12% average annual yield (reinvested). After 20 years you would have a fund worth $96,463 before tax, whether it be a buy-and-hold fund or an active-trading fund. If you sold either fund after 20 years you would end up with $62,094 after tax, assuming a 53% tax bracket (only 75% of capital gains are taxable). However, if you had owned the active-trading fund, over the years you would have had to pay income tax on its gains each year. If you didn't have cash to cover that tax liability you would have had to sell units to get it. In effect that reduces your eventual after-tax gain to an equivalent of $41,475. So you'd be better off long term with the buy-and-hold fund and philosophy.

The buy-and-hold funds appeal to us as financial professionals not only because they are tax friendly but because of their philosophy—we don't agree with a market-timing approach to creating wealth because not many people can consistently predict the peaks and valleys of the stock market over the long term.

Deferring taxes on a consistent basis takes a lot of self-discipline, since it never provides immediate gratification. Many people want their tax relief *Now*, and have a difficult time focusing 20 years down the road. To address that need for immediate tax relief and to get that shot of immediate financial adrenaline that many seem to crave, you need to be aware of every strategy available that will give you the third D: Deduct.

D THREE: DEDUCT

Some Canadians will make foolhardy investments just to get a tax deduction. Remember, however, that tax deductions often exist because there is an inherent investment risk—the government offers an incentive to stimulate investment in an otherwise risky venture. Four ways to obtain tax deductions are by using RRSPs, leveraging, labour-sponsored funds and limited partnerships.

RRSPs: tax deduction frenzy

We mentioned under the 2nd D (Defer) that you get a tax deduction when you contribute to an RRSP. This can be a significant saving. If you are in a 50% marginal tax bracket and contribute $1 to an RRSP, you will lower your tax bill by 50¢.

To maximize this deduction, be sure to take advantage of the carry-forward provision: if you contribute less than your allowable maximum in a year, you may carry forward the unused amount to later years. You might even find it would work out better for you to deliberately defer some or all of a contribution in a year so you can claim it later when you will be in a higher marginal tax rate.

There is much you should know about RRSPs before rushing in at the end of February to make a frantic deposit just to get a tax deduction. The most important factor should be how you invest that money. Consult a professional to help you make a prudent decision. Don't take RRSPs lightly—they could comprise a major portion of your retirement income.

Leveraging: be aware but don't necessarily beware

Leveraging means borrowing money for the purposes of investing. It can be a controversial strategy, but if done conservatively with the long term in mind, it can help you meet your planning goals. Many of us have used leveraging at some point but we may not have identified it that way. Have you borrowed to buy a house? That is leveraging. When you borrow (assume a mortgage) for a house, your interest costs are not tax deductible. But when you borrow to invest, the interest is deductible.

Most wealthy people use leveraging. In fact, many of them would not be wealthy had they not. There are only two forces in this world: people at work and money at work. Leveraging is a way of making your hard-earned money work as hard for you as you worked for it.

Is leveraging risky? Yes. Everything related to money is risky. If you stick it under your pillow, you take a risk that it will not grow and you thus will not keep pace with inflation. That means you could outlive your money. You run a risk owning your home. How many people are living in a house today that is worth less or no more than it was just a few years ago?

The idea is to minimize risk. You do that by diversifying and maintaining a long-term perspective. Before you contemplate leveraging, you must be sure to have the financial resources to withstand a jump in interest rates or a drop in stock-market values—you must be able to afford loan payments without hardship. Remember, leverging can magnify losses as well as profits.

Here's an example of the power of leveraging and specifically its tax advantages: Imagine two investors, Allen and Bob. They differ about how to build their long-term wealth. Each is able to invest $13,325 a year for the long term. Allen places a yearly sum into his self-directed RRSP in the form of Canadian (80%) and international (20%) equity funds. It grows at an average annual rate of 12%.

Bob, on the other hand, borrows $205,000 at an average annual interest rate of 6.5% and makes interest-only payments. He buys the same mutual funds as Allen, but outside an RRSP. Both investors receive a deduction, one from the RRSP contribution and the other from the loan interest, so there is no difference so far. But look at the difference when the two investors meet in 10 years time: Allen has a comfortable RRSP nest egg of $196,545, but Bob has an even more comfortable hoard of $636,698 (minus the $205,000 he still owes the bank, of course).

The key to Bob's success was starting with the larger sum. You may think that the RRSP should grow more quickly because of tax-free compounding. But suppose you invest the borrowed money in tax-efficient mutual funds— couldn't they increase in a tax-deferred environment as well? Keep in mind that RRSPs are restricted to 20% foreign content while non-registered funds are not. Over the long term, foreign investments have historically outper- formed Canadian investments.

Let's look, from a tax perspective, at how Allen and Bob draw income from their savings when they retire. Assume both are in a 50% marginal tax bracket. When Allen withdraws $1 from his RRSP, it costs him 50¢ in tax. When Bob takes $1 from his non-registered funds, he pays tax on the growth portion, but, by law, only 75% of it (this works out to about 37.5¢). Bob's leveraged scenario provides him with a bigger financial pot and allows him to pay less tax on an ongoing basis.

Labour-sponsored funds: do your research

An investment in labour-sponsored funds provides immediate tax relief, but you must weigh that carefully against potentially serious pitfalls. You could save 30¢ for every dollar you invest, up to a maximum in each calendar year, if the fund offers both federal and provincial tax credits. The maximum investment in a calendar year for the maximum benefit is $5,000.

If you hold these funds in an RRSP you could get back 80¢ (assuming a 50% tax bracket) for every dollar invested. Sounds almost too good to be true. But you only get the deductions once and there are restrictions. For instance, the funds must remain invested for a minimum of eight years (with a few exceptions). Read the propsectus carefully—this product is not for everybody.

Typically, these funds are poor performers. As of May 1998, a top-performing fund reported an annual, compounded return of 4.5% since its inception six years before. An investment of $5,000 in a regular mutual fund averaging 10% growth over the required holding period would have swelled to $10,718 compared to the labour-sponsored fund's $7,111. As with any investment, you must look beyond immediate tax relief to the basic quality of the fund.

Limited partnerships: do even more research

This an extensive subject and real-estate limited partnerships are not suitable for all investors. Many types are available but we will discuss only those investing in real estate because we believe that there should be an underlying investment associated with a tax shelter. Real-estate limited partnerships allow you to participate in the growth (or loss) of the underlying asset while at the same time participate in cash flow from the property—and the associated tax deductions. The deductions are generated from capital cost allowance (CCA), soft costs and mortgage/loan interest, all of which are justifiable and reasonable.

A real-estate limited partnership is like an armchair real-estate investment. The properties are professionally managed on your behalf and could produce substantial returns over time. It's important to be aware of the credentials and reputation of the syndicator who puts the deal together. A lot of people have lost money because of unscrupulous syndicators. These are complex investments and you should seek qualified professional advice before considering one—and only then if you are quite comfortable with the investment itself.

Never be afraid to seek help

If you have learned from this chapter one or two tax-reduction techniques that you weren't aware of, perhaps it will suggest to you that financial help from a qualified professional can be worthwhile. Professionals don't know everything, but they usually know where to find the answers. Don't guess about your financial future—planning eliminates most of the guesswork.

PAUL JACKSON is a partner in the Chilliwack, British Columbia, Money Concepts office. He has a BA and has completed the Canadian Securities course. He is a member of the Canadian Association of Insurance and Financial Advisors and is working towards his Certified Financial Planner (CFP) designation.

Paul, a member of the Money Concepts President's Club, is married with one son. His leisure activities include playing and coaching hockey, playing softball and travelling.

CRAIG LEHR, also a Chilliwack partner and member of the Money Concepts President's Club, is a Certified Financial Planner. He has a special interest in advanced tax planning and investment strategies. He is married, also plays and coaches hockey and enjoys golfing and fishing.

Paul and Craig's clients are average Canadians: teachers, lawyers, doctors, government employees and blue-collar workers. The partners prepare financial plans for clients at no cost and provide regular follow-ups. Their services include RRSPs, mutual funds, GICs, annuities, benefit packages and life and disability insurance. Paul and Craig may be reached by telephone at 604-795-4505, and by fax at 604-795-4816.

6

Creating Wealth Means Controlling Your Cash Flow & Ignoring Conventional Wisdom

By Allan Johnson

*T*homas and Lisa (they are friends and clients of mine) had taken advice from their parents, their banks and the media. But they weren't getting anywhere, financially. The old ways were not working and they weren't creating any wealth for retirement. Finally they asked my advice. This is the story of why they weren't getting anywhere, what they learned about their financial habits and what they finally did about it.

A few years ago they invited me to a barbecue supper. After a cappuccino and a biscotti dessert, Thomas told me, "We're both in our late 30s and we know for sure we won't have financial freedom at age 55 like the ads suggest we could. The next 10 years had better be different than the last 10. We make more than $60,000 a year but we can't save. We know we should be doing better but we don't know what to do differently."

I suggested that today's results are determined by yesterday's decisions so we needed to review what they had been doing. We agreed to get together in my office the next day to go over that.

One of the first questions I asked when they had settled down at the office was what for them was important about money, and whether they had specific goals. Lisa said, "Well, we need money to buy things that we want. We'd like to be able to help other people, too. And we would like to be financially independent."

I asked them what financial independence meant to them. Thomas answered: "We'd like to have enough money to do what we want when we want to do it."

"So how much is enough?" I said.

They didn't know. "We just want a nice home and to drive newer cars," Lisa said, "We want to maintain our standard of living when we retire."

I asked them how many months or years they could survive comfortably if they couldn't work for some reason. "I don't know," Thomas said. "How do I tell? I guess if I missed a few paycheques, I would have to start cashing in RRSPs and we only have $2,100 of them. So it wouldn't be very long. I guess I'd get some benefits from work but I'm not sure for how long."

How do you measure wealth?

I suggested to them that you measure true financial wealth by how much money your assets are able to generate for you to cover more than your expenses, indefinitely. The minimum definition of wealth is when your income covers only your expenses. But the minimum is not enough.

"You'll never earn enough money to get ahead financially if you aren't doing so with what you're earning today. We have to determine," I said, "how much you need each year to maintain your current lifestyle."

They appeared to be a typical family in a typical neighbourhood with typical jobs. Their family backgrounds are modest. As newlyweds, Thomas and Lisa were fortunate to find work in stable companies. They felt successful; their future was bright so they decided to buy a home. A condo, Lisa said. "Our parents reminded us that our home is our largest investment and our greatest asset." I did not mention to them yet that the wealthy know that a home can be a liability, and if a home is a person's largest investment, they could be in trouble.

Before long baby Elizabeth arrived. This stimulated a demand for more cash. They both offered to work overtime when possible. As their incomes increased, so did their expenses—and their income taxes.

Soon little Luke arrived to keep his sister company. Four people in a two-bedroom condo didn't seem to work so they looked for a bigger home. Their friendly banker made it very easy by pre-approving them for a substantial mortgage. The bank also offered mortgage insurance. How convenient; they just added the insurance premiums to the monthly mortgage payments. It was almost painless. The bank also agreed to pay their property taxes each year and added this cost to the monthly mortgage payments.

Thomas and Lisa then mentioned that an alert life-insurance agent spotted the birth announcements and promptly sold them two life insurance policies to protect the new arrivals.

It wasn't long before they found that two adults and two children plus the necessary paraphernalia made their Ford Escort bulge at the seams. "Like most of our friends who were also just starting out, we borrowed again from the bank for a bigger car." With two stable incomes, they qualified easily. They decided to finance the car insurance too, because the premium was a large chunk of money to come up with all at once. The insurance agent told them that many people do it because it is easier to manage with smaller, equal payments.

As the need for more income presented itself, Thomas began to moonlight at his previous trade on his days off. His income went up, but so did his tax bracket, again, something he did not notice until the following spring. Property taxes on the more-expensive home also were higher.

"As the paycheques arrived, we wondered where the money had gone," Thomas said,

They recognized the need for a short-term emergency fund. It just so happened that they were offered the opportunity to purchase Canada Savings Bonds by payroll deduction. Their employers encouraged it and the government applauded them for making such a responsible investment. It was automatic, it was painless and it helped them save. The government also guaranteed it. Fortunately for them, the CSBs matured just in time to pay off their charge cards each January because the added Christmas spending really put a drain on their bank accounts.

"As the children started school," Lisa said, "providing for their future education came to mind. Friends recommended a couple of scholarship education plans. If we started them right away, there would be enough money in time for university."

Of course the media was constantly reminding them to prepare for their own retirement because there may not be much in the government pension coffers by the time they stopped working. RRSPs seemed to be the most popular investment.

"Unfortunately," Lisa said, "we didn't have the money to contribute to RRSPs in February because it was right after Christmas, so we took out an RRSP loan from the bank. They gave us their preferred interest rate because we bought their highly recommended guaranteed investment certificates (GICs). They were guaranteed and risk-free—what a combination. We remembered our parents telling us that we shouldn't chance our hard-earned money on risky investments."

Thomas added, "It's amazing how different products and services were developed to meet our needs. We had trouble saving for holidays. The next thing we knew, we were receiving offers in the mail for our first gold credit cards and then platinum cards from a number of different banks. I guess they thought we've been responsible with our finances and our use of credit so we are the kind of people they want to do business with. We feel pleased about the good credit rating we have established. We can even buy groceries on our cards now. We don't have to worry whether we have money in our accounts because we have a great credit rating."

Cash flow should not be all outwards

By this time I had identified 15 areas where Thomas and Lisa could make significant changes to the way they manage their cash flow. I told them cash flow is king and that if they were ever going to control their financial life, they needed to control their cash flow first.

One of the major problems people have, I told my friends, when managing (or not managing) their cash flow is the quality and source of the advice they act upon. There is a lot of advice around, much of it well-intentioned and from the educated majority. A better source is to study what the wealthy do–those who have succeeded financially. You will find that they have followed a fairly specific path. It may be a path you are not familiar with, or even comfortable with at the beginning. If you want to travel this path, you likely will have to change your habits and attitudes–the path will not change to fit you.

"We want to make a change," Thomas and Lisa said, "but we don't know what to do. We generally followed our parents' advice and that of the experts they consulted, such as the bank. This doesn't seem to be working."

"It's a system that might have worked at one time," I answered, "but does it work today? I don't think it does, do you? You followed it and you are not what we usually think of as independently wealthy. There are a lot of reasons for this."

One of them, I remarked, is credit-card companies. Naturally, they are in business to make money and that's why they offer you an easy opportunity to get deeper into debt. You should only use charge cards for travel or emergencies, not for fixed or regular living expenses. And you should try to pay them off in full each month. Use cash for your basic living expenses.

Another reason you have been having trouble getting ahead financially is that you have never formally learned how to manage money. That's not surprising: the schools don't teach it. Most of what we know came from our parents. And middle-class parents don't have the best credentials for teaching their children about money management—it wasn't a school subject when they attended. Neither, for that matter, were subjects such as being a spouse, raising children, shopping for a mortgage, understanding life insurance, balancing a cheque book or investing for retirement. Even after 12 years of school and four years of university most of us are not well equipped to handle life's basic experiences that we face as adults.

"Perhaps," said Thomas, "that's why some of my friends who are well-educated professionals like doctors, dentists, accountants and lawyers struggle financially along with the rest of the working population."

I agreed and added, "it could also account for some of our staggering provincial and national debts. Our often highly educated politicians and government officials make critical financial decisions with little or no training in the subject of money management."

This is a principal reason for the incredibly fast and strong growth of the financial planning industry, I suggested. It meets an increasing need for financial education.

Thomas asked, "Speaking about parents, what about my dad advising me to pay all of our bills first and keep or save what's left?" I told him, "The wealthy pay themselves first and then pay their bills. We must learn to spend within our means."

Lisa said, "My dad always told me to study hard, get your diploma and you will get a good job." I said, "The wealthy would encourage you to get a diploma, but also to study how to create wealth. You must understand how money works and learn how money can work for you."

It's generally accepted that wealthy Canadians make up 10% of the population and own the majority of the shares of corporate Canada. The other 90% lends its money to the banks and governments. Owners make the real money. Lenders tend to be fearful and overly conservative.

"My parents," Thomas said, "taught us that when it comes to money, play it safe, don't take risks." I responded, "The wealthy learn to manage risk by understanding their investments."

Money alone won't solve people's problems. Money without a financial education is money soon gone. How many times have you heard stories of lottery winners or professional athletes who are suddenly rich, and then sooner or later poor again. We live in a society structured to help you and your money part company unless you are trained to handle it properly. Grant Sylvester said it so well in his financial planning book, *The Money Jar*: "Most people don't plan to fail, they just fail to plan."

Owning assets is the key

So what do you study? What do you learn? Who do you listen to? Who is right? You begin with the basics. The first thing is to learn the difference between an asset and a liability. Ask yourself this: Does your investment put money in your pocket or take money out of it? If you want to be wealthy, spend your lifetime buying assets. But you have to know what you are doing—many people acquire liabilities and they think they are assets.

Assets create wealth. Let's go back to the home-ownership issue. The home is a liability even if it is fully paid for because it continually takes money out of your pocket: mortgage payments, property taxes, insurance, maintenance and utilities. If all of your money is tied up in your house, where does your retirement income come from? You will always need a place to live and that will cost money whether you rent or own. But you might want to go out for supper once in a while or take a holiday. This requires additional income. You need shelter, but don't tie up all your money in it.

Assets should generate more than enough income to cover expenses. Then, reinvested surplus income buys more assets. As the assets grow, so does income. Let your assets purchase luxuries. That's the kind of treadmill to get on rather than the one you are on now, I suggested to Thomas and Lisa.

"But where can we find the money to buy assets?" Thomas said. "We're tapped out right now on two full-time incomes and a part-time job." By keeping more of what you earn, I told them.

I asked what their biggest expenses were. Lisa answered, "Our mortgage and car payments." "Not really," I said, and pointed out that taxes account for a larger share: income tax, property tax, school tax, sales tax and social services taxes. Thomas admitted that they had never calculated the impact of taxes on their cash flow. "What can we do about it?" he asked.

"We all have to pay taxes." I said, "But one of the first things we will do to improve your cash flow is reduce the amount of tax you pay. It's quite legal to *minimize* the tax you pay by restructuring your financial affairs. Tax *evasion*, of course, is illegal."

"I pay the same income tax as my buddies at work," Thomas said. "How can I change that? Most of my income is wages." I explained that one way was to depart from what he has always done: he should file an L-18 form (Reduction of Income Tax at Source) with Revenue Canada, which would allow his employer to reduce his income-tax payroll deduction immediately. But first, we needed to structure his financial affairs so that he would be in a position to use this strategy.

"Have you ever noticed," I asked the couple, "that the safer your investment (such as GICs), the higher it's taxed? The more debt you have, the more you pay the bank. The more things you own, the more things you need to insure. It's pretty clear that a lot of your money goes to Revenue Canada, the banks and the insurance companies—unnecessarily.

"It's my job to help you figure out how to keep more of what you earn."

One way is to do what the wealthy do: as often as possible, choose investments that generate capital gains or dividend income instead of interest income . Both of these attract a lower tax rate than interest income, or wages for that matter.

As Grant Sylvester wrote, "it's not how much money you make, but what you do with what you make that determines how well and how quickly you create wealth."

Why not earn income as you sleep?

There is nothing more comforting than going to bed at night knowing your investment will be earning money for you as you sleep. When you do invest in assets, there are three considerations necessary to maximize your efforts:

1. Time. The longer you let your money work for you, the more advantage you can take from the power of compounding.

2. Taxes. Be aware of the impact taxes have on your ability to create wealth. Include tax-efficient investments as part of your strategy.

3. Growth. Since you are after growth, use only investments that are likely to provide it. Your investments must not have a cap or lid on how much they can increase.

To create wealth by investing, you must understand how investments work. Investing is money making money (for you). Your investment will go up and down as the stock market fluctuates, but the overall trend is up. It's a long-term concept and there are risks along the way. But you learn to manage risk as you go.

The inability of people to handle risk is one reason more of them are not wealthy. The fear of losing capital is widespread. The critical variable in successful investing is investor behaviour, not investment performance. Many well-intentioned advisors suggest that investors play it safe, diversify and include a lot of secure investments. This might be a balanced portfolio that includes money-market instruments and some bonds and corporate shares. This definitely qualifies as a safe and sensible portfolio and caters to the fears of the average investor. But this conservative, balanced, diversified investment portfolio is designed more to avoid losing money than to make it grow. This is what perhaps 90% of investors do and it's why that 90% is not wealthy, or likely to be.

The majority is advised not to put all its eggs in one basket. But if you want to be among the 10% of investors who create significant wealth, you must be sharply focused in your selection of investments. You must put more eggs in fewer baskets. Through mutual funds, invest in a selection of excellent businesses that dominate their share of the market and have the potential for long-term growth. This strategy is not for the meek; you must be willing to accept the ups and downs on this path to financial freedom, including some rough spots that could break an egg or two. The success of any investment comes from two primary sources: the quality of investment and the length of time you hold it. The road to success isn't always smooth. If it were, everyone would take it. When you use money to make money, you won't get any guarantees. But there is tremendous potential to generate great returns.

What you know will be your greatest asset. What you don't know will be your greatest risk. How do you know what you don't know? Your own intelligence and experience plus the experience of a capable advisor should hold you in good stead. There will always be risk when investing. The challenge is to learn to manage risk instead of avoiding it. If you start investing at an early age, you already have reduced your risk substantially because you have time on your side to recover from any setbacks.

A successful seven-year journey

Most of us get a lot of advice; only the wise profit from it. But the most valuable advice in the world is useless unless you implement it. Thomas and Lisa did take action after I analyzed their financial habits and drew up a financial plan they could follow. Here is where they started seven years ago and where they are today:

IN 1991 THEY HAD:	IN 1998 THEY HAD:
2-bedroom condo with mortgage	3-bedroom, 3-bathroom home
1976 Buick, and car loan payments	1992 Isuzu pickup, paid for
1982 Ford Escort and loan payments	1993 Intrepid, paid for
$2,150 in RRSPs and a bank loan	$123,000 in RRSP investments
	$10,000 sideline business
	$50,000 business partnership
	Bank line of credit

That's a long way down the road towards financial independence. They have created a lot of wealth. Here is how they did it (keep in mind that not everything they did is suitable for other investors):

♦ 1991. Sold the condo and bought a three-bedroom, three-bathroom home.

♦ 1991. Stopped financing property taxes. Saved for it in advance.

♦ 1991. Started to invest in RRSPs monthly, reducing income taxes.

♦ 1992. Stopped buying CSBs through payroll deduction.

♦ 1992. Dropped children's life insurance and applied money to RRSPs.

♦ 1992. Replaced mortgage and loan insurance with life insurance.

♦ 1992. Thomas set up a home-based business; ran it on his days off.

♦ 1992. Bought an Isuzu pickup for the business so it was tax deductible.

♦ 1994. Increased the size of the house mortgage and used the money to buy a duplex. The interest was a deductible expense.

♦ 1994. Established a low-interest bank line of credit.

♦ 1994. Bought a new 1993 Chrysler Intrepid with cash.

♦ 1994. Borrowed $20,000 from the bank for investment purposes using the car as collateral, so the interest cost was tax deductible. If they had financed the car, the loan interest would not be deductible.

◆ 1994. The rental property and business expenses, deductible investment-loan interest and RRSP contributions all reduced income taxes substantially.

◆ 1996. Sold duplex for $20,000 profit and paid down line of credit.

◆ 1996. Purchased a Real Estate Limited Partnership (LP) for $17,500. Borrowed the money and paid interest only. This results in additional tax deductions for the next five years and a potential profit of $25,000.

◆ 1996. Thomas filed an L-18 to reduce his income taxes at the source. He had no paycheque income-tax deductions from September to December. He used this saving to maximize his RRSPs for the year. His work mates were in disbelief and told him that he was going to jail. Of course Thomas did nothing illegal, so he had the last laugh.

◆ 1997. Employer offered Lisa a voluntary separation package.

◆ 1998. Lisa became a partner and owner in her own marketing business. Thomas does some work for her and now shares his wife's office, thus reducing costs.

Thomas and Lisa learned many small lessons that when combined, made a huge difference over the past seven years. Here are some they told me about:

◆ In general, if something may possibly appreciate in value, consider owning it. If it will depreciate, rent or lease it. Definitely look into this distinction before buying another vehicle.

◆ Bank some of every paycheque to save for next year's insurance premiums—it's too expensive to finance them with borrowed money.

◆ Do the same for Christmas expense money.

◆ Consider switching from scholarship education plans (RESPs) to joint accounts and in-trust accounts instead. There are a lot of rules, regulations and conditions in RESPs so that in effect someone else has control of your money.

◆ Contribute directly to your own RRSPs rather than borrowing from the bank. Interest on an RRSP loan is not tax deductible. Cut down on the use of credit cards.

◆ Borrow to buy investments, not to acquire consumables.

Thomas and Lisa have indeed come a long way, and they continue to learn about managing their own money. I still learn too, and I can pass on what I learn to friends and to clients. That makes financial planning a satisfying profession for me.

ALLAN JOHNSON is president of Money Concepts in Prince George, British Columbia. He has studied how financially successful people create their wealth, and incorporates this knowledge into the financial-planning process that he uses for the benefit of a wide range of clients.

He considers his profession especially gratifying because he is doing what he loves and at the same time he helps improve the financial lives of clients. His firm offers comprehensive financial-planning services including estate, retirement and investment planning, and access to wide range of financial products, such as mutual funds, RRSPs and life and disability insurance.

Allan helps clients define clear goals and incorporates these into a planning process that allows them to achieve their aspirations and dreams. "By providing financial peace of mind, we help create a desirable balance of health, wealth and happiness."

Allan's background includes the forest industry, real estate, small business and the fire service. He is and has been a volunteer for countless organizations in Prince George including coaching amateur sports, the Rotary Club, the Knights of Columbus, the Prince George Hospice Society and is active in his church with his wife, Anita, leading marriage-preparation courses.

Allan and Anita enjoy spending time with their three sons. Allan may be reached by telephone at 250-564-7484 and by fax at 250-563-3281. His website is www.moneyconceptspg.bc.ca and his e-mail is aj@moneyconceptspg.bc.ca.

7

Borrowing to Invest

The DOs and DON'Ts of leveraging   By David H. Karas
CFP, RFP

*L*everaging (borrowing to invest) is an aspect of financial planning that is subject to more sacred-cow mythology than any other. Sacred cows—otherwise known as blindly accepted values—not only have a high maintenance cost, but they rarely provide any benefits. Somebody, for some reason, wrote away back when that an individual's ultimate financial objective should be to be completely debt free by the time retirement rolls around. Too many people today believe this implicitly though it is no longer valid in today's society. They thus jeopardize their retirement years and dreams of a secure financial future.

Leverage makes sense when . . .

 ♦   you have brain-dead capital not earning much for you. Putting all of your assets to work will increase your overall return.
 ♦   you are a disciplined investor and you establish a debt/equity ratio you can comfortably live with, consistent with your tolerance for risk.
 ♦   you are in a higher tax bracket. The higher the tax bracket the more help you get from the tax department if you use leverage.
 ♦   you stick with lower-volatility mutual funds to minimize the effect of market swings.

Some financial pundits believe that borrowing money to invest is too risky for the average investor because if the investment does poorly, or loses value, you still have to repay the loan. But I am a long-time believer in the prudent use of debt because there are times when borrowing to invest makes a great deal of sense. Remember, leverage works both ways: profit and loss.

At one time I referred to unused assets as "stagnant pools of capital," but now I think the term "brain-dead capital" is a more appropriate description. Brain-dead capital in my lexicon is money tied up in assets that don't produce income, have little or no growth prospects above the level of inflation and cost you money to keep secure, insure and maintain. Thousands of dollars sitting in a bank account is a perfect example.

Examples of assets that are brain-dead capital

- ◆ house/condo
- ◆ cottage
- ◆ motor home
- ◆ weekend farm
- ◆ boat
- ◆ vacant land and lots
- ◆ expensive car
- ◆ bloated bank accounts

Assign a realistic value to each asset, add them up and compare the total to your revenue-producing assets (usually investments such as mutual funds, stocks and bonds). Don't be surprised to find that more than half or even up to 60% of your total assets produce no revenue, show minimum growth and cost you money. In some cases the percentage may be as high as 70% to 75%. In other words, 25% to 40% of your assets are being asked to support the remaining 60% to 75% of your wealth. Let's look at a few ways to put more assets to work and swing the odds more in your favour.

BORROWING AGAINST YOUR HOME

The biggest single asset most people acquire is their home. Let's tackle the prevailing attitude about paying off your home as quickly as possible so that in 20 to 25 years you are mortgage free. Great, you've done it. Now what do you do? You've been flinging money at your mortgage in the form of extra payments, you have some RRSPs, but you have very little other available capital. This is one of life's most ridiculous situations—asset-rich and cash-poor. poor. You have practically no cash money for discretionary spending but you've got $200,000 tied up in real estate that provides nothing but free rent, and costs you taxes, fuel and maintenance to keep it going.

You could sell the house and use the proceeds for investment purposes. You move into a rental property and pay the rent from salary or self-employed income, or use the income produced by the investment. But those who wish the peace of mind of staying in their own homes need only to borrow against the value of the house. You then invest the loan in revenue-producing assets.

This approach can do a lot for you. First and foremost it means the money you have handed over to the mortgage company for 20 years or so can now create an income for you in retirement. The objective is to generate enough revenue from the investment to pay the cost of the mortgage and leave some surplus that will grow and compound when you invest it wisely. The government will help you do this because the interest on the loan is tax deductible (Revenue Canada will pay up to 53% of the loan interest cost for you, depending on your tax bracket).

To just stay even with the game when you take the money out of the home and invest it, the investment has to grow only at the rate the house would have gained in value over time, plus the net cost of the investment loan. Today, for most people, the net cost of an investment loan is between 3% and 4% at most. If real estate continues to deflate as it has been, then you only need to cover that net loan cost to stay even. Anything your investment earns beyond the cost of the loan, plus inflation, is a profit.

Take a look at the first table on the next page (*Home Ownership vs. Equity Investment*). It demonstrates how much more you can end up with (even paying rent for a similar home) by selling a $200,000 home that you would expect to increase in value at 3% per year, compared to investing the home-sale proceeds in equity investments that give you 12% return. Tax liability is not accounted for in this illustration. The exact amount would depend upon whether the growth is a capital gain, dividend or straight interest.

If you did nothing and left the money in the house and if the house grew in value by 3% a year, you would, of course, still increase in your net worth. But you would not be able to use it. It's a pretty poor return that you can't get your hands on. I tell many of my retired clients that if they don't spend the money represented by their house while they are alive, I guarantee someone else will spend it successfully after they are dead.

HOME OWNERSHIP VS. EQUITY INVESTMENT

Initial investment amount (and value of home): $200,000.00
Years invested: 20

Primary residence not subject to capital gains tax			Investment gains will be taxable	
Home value grows at 3% per year			Equity investment grows at 12% per year	
YEAR	GROWTH	TOTAL VALUE	ANNUAL GROWTH	TOTAL VALUE
1	$6,000	$206,000	$24,000	$224,000
2	6,180	212,180	26,880	250,880
3	6,365	218,545	30,106	280,986
4	6,556	225,102	33,718	314,704
5	6,753	231,854	37,764	352,468
6	6,956	238,810	42,296	394,765
7	7,164	245,975	47,372	442,136
8	7,379	253,354	53,056	495,193
9	7,601	260,954	59,423	554,616
10	7,829	268,783	66,554	621,170
11	8,064	276,847	74,540	695,710
12	8,306	285,152	83,485	779,195
13	8,555	293,407	93,503	872,699
14	8,811	302,518	104,724	977,422
15	9,076	311,593	117,291	1,094,713
16	9,348	320,941	131,366	1,226,079
17	9,628	330,569	147,129	1,373,208
18	9,917	340,486	164,785	1,537,993
19	10,215	350,701	184,559	1,722,552
20	10,521	361,222	206,706	1,929,259
	$161,222	$361,222	$1,729,259	$1,929,259

The information contained herein is based on certain assumptions and is for illustration purposes only. While care is taken in the preparation of this document no warranty is made as to its accuracy or applicability in any particular case.

Reluctant to sell? Try a line of credit

I suggest to clients who don't want to sell their homes, that they get a bank line of credit. As I write this you can get a secured loan of credit for 4.75%, using your home as collateral. Most institutions will allow you up to 70% of the value of the $200,000 house so that's the amount we use in our next illustration: $140,000. We assume in the second table, on the facing page (*Line of Credit–Basic*), that the cost of borrowing is 8%–much higher than today's actual cost, so this scenario is ultra conservative and includes a big fudge factor in case rates increase. You

LINE OF CREDIT—BASIC

Borrow $140,000 against home and invest in equities for 20 years.
Loan cost is 8% and you withdraw $550.67 monthly from the investment to cover the
NET cost of the loan. WITHDRAWAL column is cumulative.

	Investment grows at 8% annually		Investment grows at 12% annually	
YEAR	WITHDRAWAL	BALANCE	WITHDRAWAL	BALANCE
1	$6,608	$144,309	$6,608	$149,770
2	13,216	148,963	13,216	160,712
3	19,824	153,989	19,824	172,967
4	26,432	159,417	26,432	186,693
5	33,040	165,279	33,040	202,067
6	39,648	171,610	39,648	219,284
7	46,256	178,448	46,256	238,568
8	52,864	185,833	52,864	260,166
9	59,472	193,809	59,472	284,356
10	66,080	202,422	66,080	311,449
11	72,688	211,725	72,688	341,793
12	79,296	221,772	79,296	375,778
13	85,905	232,623	85,905	413,841
14	92,513	244,342	92,513	456,472
15	99,121	256,998	99,121	504,218
16	105,729	270,667	105,729	557,694
17	112,337	285,429	112,337	617,587
18	118,945	301,372	118,945	684,668
19	125,553	318,571	125,553	759,798
20	$132,161	$337,187	$132,161	$843,943
	$132,161	**$337,187**	**$132,161**	**$843,943**

The information contained herein is based on certain assumptions and is for illustration purposes only. While care is taken in the preparation of this document no warranty is made as to its accuracy or applicability in any particular case.

invest the loan proceeds and use the income it earns to pay the net monthly loan interest cost ($550.67). In the table, loan interest is entitled *Withdrawal*.

The loan cost in this table is the *net* interest cost only—the after-tax cost. You must apply to revenue Canada for permission for your employer to reduce the amount of tax deducted each month from your paycheque because of the deductible amount of interest you are paying. It is deductible because you use the loan for non-RRSP investment purposes. We use a tax rate of 41% for this illustration and 8% and also 12% annually as examples of a range of investment returns you might expect, from modest to good.

Even if your investment earned only 8% annually, after 10 years you would have a retirement fund of $202,402. At a 12% return you would have $311,449, and although we don't have enough space to show it, a 15% return would leave you with $421,542 stashed away for your golden years. After 20 years the totals would be a lot more. If you wanted extra money at any time you could take out a lump sum, especially if there was strong growth from a good stock-market year. Even in a year when your investment, presumably mutual funds, does not earn the interest cost, you could still take some money from the principal. The investment wouldn't grow as quickly in that case, but if you give it a while to recover it will soon be back to the original amount.

The third table, shown below (*Line of Credit–Advanced*), is essentially the same scenario, except that you are withdrawing an additional $600 a month ($7,200 a year) over and above the cost of the loan, to spend as you like. The total net withdrawal is no more than 10% of the total principal so you may use the free-unit withdrawals allowed by mutual funds if you bought them on a deferred-sales-charge basis. Under this option (DSC) you are allowed 10% free withdrawal a year (no commissions payable). The amount varies among fund companies but most abide by the 10% standard. So, you have an additional $7,200 a year to spend and the net interest payments have all been made on the house loan. Keep in mind that in this illustration, the 8% loan cost is higher than actual rates when this was written, so the scenario is conservative. Rates should remain quite low well into the first decade of the new century. We have abbreviated the table because of space limitations.

LINE OF CREDIT—ADVANCED

Borrow $140,000 against home and invest in equities for 20 years.
Loan cost is 8% and you withdraw $550.67 monthly from the investment to cover the
NET cost of the loan, PLUS $600 extra spending money per month. WITHDRAWAL
column is cumulative.

	Investment grows at 8% annually		Investment grows at 12% annually	
YEAR	WITHDRAWAL	BALANCE	WITHDRAWAL	BALANCE
1	$13,808	$136,801	$13,808	$142,110
2	27,616	133,345	27,616	144,473
5	69,040	121,231	69,040	153,404
10	138,080	93,652	138,080	177,027
15	207,121	53,131	207,121	218,659
20	$269,885	$0	$276,161	$292,029
	$269,885	**$0**	**$276,161**	**$292,029**

The information contained herein is based on certain assumptions and is for illustration purposes only. While care is taken in the preparation of this document no warranty is made as to its accuracy or applicability in any particular case.

BORROWING TO MAKE AN RRSP CONTRIBUTION.

In past years borrowing to make an RRSP contribution was an attractive idea, especially since you were allowed to deduct the interest cost from your taxable income. Today you cannot deduct the interest, but if you act prudently you may still profit from an RRSP loan. One of the best illustrations of this point is made in the book *The Money Jar* by the late Grant Sylvester, co-founder of Money Concepts Canada:

First, you should be able to afford the monthly payments–principal and interest–with no difficulty. Second, you must be able to pay off your loan within a year. If you can't pay it off within that time, don't borrow. You'll send yourself into an upward spiral of debt that could spin you right into bankruptcy.

This is how it works: assume your income allows you to make a contribution of $4,000 this year. You borrow the $4,000 at a fixed rate of 15%, which is compounded yearly [Ed. note: this was written several years ago when interest rates were much higher]. *Your monthly interest and principal payments (based on paying off the loan in 1 year or less) are $312.40. You are in a 40% tax bracket, so your $4,000 contribution qualifies you for a tax rebate of $1,600. You use the rebate to pay down your loan principal (say, for sake of argument, 3 months after you take out the loan). You maintain the same monthly payments, which means the loan is paid off after about 8 months. Over this period you have paid $204 in interest out of your pocket.*

In the meantime the $4,000 contribution is earning interest in the RRSP at, say, 11%, and this builds up in a tax-deferred environment for the year. That amounts to $440 for the year. So, at the end of the year you have earned $236 (pre-tax) in interest more than you have paid out, your loan is completely paid off and your $4,000 plus the $440 interest will continue to grow, tax-free, for many years until you mature the RRSP.

This borrowing scenario works. Most others don't. Approach the idea with caution.

Most people make their annual RRSP contribution just before deadline time at the end of February, often in a lump sum using borrowed funds. The problem with doing this is that it always leaves you one year behind and you lose that full year's investment earnings. It would be better to make your RRSP contribution at the start of the tax year, or at least monthly as the year progresses. That way you earn interest, dividends and growth earlier and that extra will compound to a much larger amount as time goes by.

No time like the present

This is an excellent time to be aggressive about investing, and borrowing to invest is aggressive. The current economic environment of low interest rates and surging equities (despite the fallback in mid-1998) can create much higher returns than GICs, money-market funds or even balanced mutual funds. The potential for meaningful profit lies in capital appreciation, and that means equity-based mutual fund investments.

The combination of borrowed money and equities is not conservative. It is essential to seek competent advice when embarking on a program like this. And watch your borrowed money like a hawk—if something goes wrong, you, not just your advisor, could be responsible.

The David Karas rules for investing borrowed capital

If you use borrowed money for investment purposes, I recommend you stick to mutual funds unless you are an expert in the evaluation of individual stocks. This said, the large number of people starting to use leverage to buy mutual funds concerns me. Remember, leverage may magnify your profits, but it may also inflate your losses. My concern is focused on the quality of financial and investment advice they are getting. For their benefit and that of my own clients, I have devised the following strategic rules:

1.   Try to use borrowed capital for investments different from those you would normally place in your RRSPs.

2.   Use borrowed money to buy more aggressive and somewhat more volatile investments than those in your RRSPs. Since you will be paying interest on the borrowed money, you should expect a higher rate of return than from a conservative RRSP, and a higher return is associated with higher risk and volatility.

3.   Diversify by asset. Never place all of your invested capital in a single mutual fund. I continue to be amazed when I see proposals from financial advisors proposing that their clients borrow $100,000 and stick it all in XYZ Far East Fund, or ABC Gold Fund or Hot Fund of the Week. Always break your capital down into three or four pools, and pick three or four of the best fund managers in each pool. A good average is a $10,000 limit per fund if you are investing $100,000. This forces you to divest.

4.   Diversify by manager type: market timer; asset allocator; sector rotator; bottom fisher; pension fund manager.

5.   Diversify geographically. Never place all your borrowed capital in just one region of the world. The most frequent poor advice that new financial advisors give clients has to do with over-weighting. For example, if you were over-weighted in the Far East at the end of December 1993 to mid-January 1994, you would have suffered immediate and significant losses.

6.   Never go to maximum exposure, or full leverage. Always leave yourself a 25% buffer of cash or available credit. You must protect yourself from the possibility of a margin call if you are using funds borrowed from a financial institution. For example, if your mutual-fund investment is collateral and the market drops, the value of the mutual fund may no longer be sufficient to cover the loan, so the bank could ask you for more cash to secure the loan. Or you could come across a further investment opportunity that you cannot exploit if you don't have the extra capital available.

7.   When you are unsure of market peaks, use dollar-cost averaging (set-amount, monthly instalments) to buy investments over a period of time. This can range from three weeks to three months or longer.

8.   Be very wary of cascading. Cascading means that you have made a profit and now are able to borrow *more* money, using the profit as collateral. This can be extremely profitable but you are at serious risk if you remain vertically integrated. For example, if you borrowed $100,000 for Canadian equities last summer and made a $40,000 profit, you would now have a portfolio worth $140,000. Let's assume you are comfortable with the increased risk of expanding your exposure and are now prepared to borrow and invest another $40,000, which your lending institution is pleased to do. If you also place this additional money in Canadian equities, you are cascading. It's risky because you now owe more money than before, and you have it all in just one segment of the market. A better idea would be to take your $40,000 profit and move it to mortgage-backed securities. Then borrow the additional funds. Diversifying the additional $40,000 in the Far East, or another alternative market, will lower your risk even more.

9. Profit-strip regularly (take your profits) and then re-balance your portfolio. Do not lose sight of the importance of maintaining balanced ratios of stocks to bonds, international to Canadian investments. Always integrate the value of your leveraged funds when you review your total assets.

10. Decide ahead of time when you are going to sell leveraged investments—and stick to that decision. Have pre-set levels, or limits, as to the cost of borrowed money, increases in portfolio value and the time available to monitor and mange your assets.

11. When working with an advisor and borrowed funds, make sure you have regular meetings, no less than once every 12 weeks. Borrowed capital is not a fire-and-forget scenario. It requires close monitoring and selective management. Make sure you get regular, consolidated reports—you cannot manage what you cannot measure.

DAVID H. KARAS, CFP, RFP, is president of the world's number-one Money Concepts office, located in Barrie, Ontario. Since 1994 he has been recognized as the top producer worldwide for the entire Money Concepts international financial-planning network. A noted editorial contributor to more than 17 newspapers and national publications, David has written two books about financial planning, and is an established commentator on financial issues both on radio and television in central and southern Ontario.

David is married to his business partner, Wendy. They have three children and are strong supporters of many charitable causes. David's favourite admonition to clients is, "Don't live poor to die rich."

He accepts new clients regularly and may be reached by telephone at 1-800-870-8522 and by fax at 705-739-7752.

8

Life Insurance Critical to Advanced Estate Planning

By Lise M. Allin, B.Sc., MPA, CLU, CHFC, CFP
& Richard Kizell, BA, CLU, RFP, CFP

*M*ost people would like to ensure the orderly transfer of their business or personal assets to heirs at death, with a minimum of delay and at its full value. Richard Kizell discusses the business side of this process and adds a couple of case histories. Lise Allin outlines methods of estate conservation and passing along personal assets when death occurs after retirement.

The strategies outlined here are somewhat sophisticated. You should discuss them with your own financial, legal and accounting advisors before attempting to implement any of them.

THE BUSINESS SIDE OF ESTATE PLANNING

Many small businesses are either incorporated and involve partnerships, or are family businesses with inter-generational shareholders. These companies are often asset-rich but cash-poor. Estate planning for small business can be a bit complicated and a financial planner must summon all the tools available and apply years of training to provide solutions.

It's often a team effort

A financial planner is often only one component of the solution; it may require a team of experts. Members could include a lawyer and an accountant, both specializing in tax. The financial planner will uncover an estate-planning challenge and, if appropriate, encourage the client to involve the lawyer and accountant. In many cases, the planner will act as team coordinator. The lawyer is invaluable in drafting legal agreements that work properly. The accountant will run various tax scenarios to find the best solution for the client and to make sure the financial planning and legal pieces fit together.

The following two case studies are real, not theoretical. Each had a unique set of challenges and solutions. In both cases the lawyer and the accountant were integral parts of the process.

Case study number one

Two unrelated individuals wanted to form a partnership within a corporation. Each would own 50% of the new firm. The partners consulted their own lawyers and accountants. The financial planner encouraged them to complete their agreements and sign them before starting business. The planner also ensured that the agreements were properly funded and protected with appropriate insurance.

There are only four things that can happen to end an active partnership:

1. One partner might decide to quit.
2. One partner could become disabled.
3. One partner could retire.
4. One partner could die.

This deal was an equal partnership with each partner owning 50 of the 100 shares issued. The shareholder's agreement provided by the lawyers stated that if the two partners could not agree, the partnership would be dissolved and one partner would purchase the shares of the other.

This could be effected by a shotgun buy-sell agreement. The idea was to prevent either partner from being able to buy out the other at an unfairly low price. The partner who wants out must name a price for the shares. The other partner may then sell at that price, or has the option to buy out the first partner *at the same price*. This helps keep the price fair, no matter who ends up with all the shares.

Despite some differences between the lawyers, the deal was signed and sealed before the business began operating. Possible issues and challenges should be on the table and dealt with before the fact, not after, especially when good will is at its highest level. If shareholders procrastinate putting agreements into place, it only gets tougher and more contentious to complete them as time passes.

As the shareholder's agreement is being formalized, the lawyer will concentrate on the legal language to get the agreement right. The financial planner in the meantime will propose solutions about funding the different aspects of the agreement.

Back up the agreement with added protection

In this case, each shareholder took out a $100,000 term-to-100 life insurance policy on the other. The agreement called for a surviving shareholder to buy the shares of a shareholder who died, and this policy was designed to allow that to happen without undue financial hardship. If the company didn't have much cash on hand, borrowing would load it or the surviving partner with debt—an unsatisfactory solution. Life insurance was the cheapest, quickest and most efficient way to provide cash to buy back the shares. The family of the deceased shareholder would have the cash they needed, and the surviving shareholder could continue the business without added debt. Without the buy-back clause, the deceased shareholder's spouse and perhaps children would otherwise still own shares in the business and be entitled to 50% of the profits. But they would not be actively contributing to the business.

Further protection

The shareholders went a step further to protect themselves. They bought disability buy-out insurance on each other. This is not a common type of insurance, but the planner made the partners realize that there was more likelihood of one of them becoming disabled than dying. Canada Life statistics from 1996 show that in any given year, one in 88 homes catch fire; one in 29 vehicles are involved in an accident, and one in 10 people are disabled. It is a difficult situation if a partner becomes disabled; the business usually depends on both partners working. The most satisfactory solution is to buy out the partner who cannot work. The disability buy-out insurance provides the cash for that scenario. The healthy partner can continue the business without having to carry a non-contributing, disabled partner, and sidesteps the necessity of adding to debt to buy the disabled partner out. The disabled partner gets a lump sum for his shares and may continue on with life.

This was a relatively simple, almost textbook case. The shareholders put agreements into place before they started the business. The key to making the deal feasible was that the insurance would ensure that the agreements could be carried out. If death or disability occurred and money was not available, the agreements might not be worth the paper they were written on. Fortunately, the partners remained healthy and became financially successful without having to call upon their shareholder's agreement.

Case study number two

Another case that illustrates useful estate-planning techniques for small business involved a father of three children. He was successful in real estate and wanted to minimize taxes so he could pass his assets on to the next generation as efficiently as possible upon his death. The problem surfaced during the preparation of an estate plan for him: there was not enough life insurance to cover potential tax liability, and that liability was growing exponentially with time.

Tax lawyers and accountants applied themselves to the problem. They recommended that the father institute an estate freeze and a Section 86 rollover under the Income Tax Act. The father exchanged his common shares in the company that he owned for preferred shares with a fixed value. He gave the three children each an equal number of common shares with a starting value of $1 each.

Professionals then evaluated the company's worth and that value was assigned to the father's preferred shares. He now knew exactly what the company was worth on the day of the freeze. So did Revenue Canada and this would avoid arguments about the value of the father's estate later on.

The evaluation also set exactly the amount of tax liability that would be owing on these new preferred shares in the event of a sale or the father's death. The freeze meant that tax liability to his estate would not grow any larger, because from that time on all of growth would flow to the common shares held by the children.

The father's shares were voting shares and there were more of them than common shares. So the father retained voting control. He continued to take a salary from the company, and received dividends from the preferreds. He also had the option of redeeming shares if he wanted more income. Also, he could redeem the preferred shares gradually over a long period of time so that the tax impact would be spread out and likely less.

Having four shareholders certainly is more complicated than one and this could be a problem. The three children would eventually own all the shares but they would not necessarily be involved in the business. If one of them died, the situation would be further complicated. To help minimize this, they decided that none of the shares would pass to any existing grandchildren until the original shareholder (the father) died.

Insurance gets around potential tax liability

The children also signed a shareholder's agreement that stipulated that if any of the children died, that (adult) child's estate was required to sell its shares to the two surviving adult children shareholders. Since real estate companies are notorious for being asset-rich but cash-poor, this could mean the company or the surviving shareholders might have to sell property to raise the cash to buy back the shares. That, however, could trigger a tax liability. The simplest and cheapest solution was for the three new common shareholders to buy life insurance on one another's lives. If one shareholder died, the other two could use the proceeds of the insurance policy to buy back the shares of their late sibling and, incidentally, compensate his family.

At first glance, this process seemed to be very complicated. But as the lawyer, the accountant and the financial planner started fitting the pieces together, it became very simple. They considered the worst-case scenarios then designed shareholder's agreements to accommodate. The financial planner had started it all by reviewing the original shareholder's estate plan with him, thus motivating him to confront the looming problem. In the end, the insurance products the planner provided would provide the cash to ensure that the agreements could be carried through.

A side issue was the father's uninsurability because of health problems. A tax liability remained on the preferred shares should they be liquidated. Since shares may pass tax free to one's spouse, the solution was to place an adequate amount of life insurance on the mother. The proceeds would pay any tax when ultimately the preferreds passed through her estate.

In both of these cases, the businesses were viable and profitable. We used a team approach (lawyer, accountant and financial planner) to come up with solutions during good times, which would avoid hostility, tax impact and confusion during the tough times. It's important to note that the cost of the insurance in both cases was a tiny fraction of what otherwise would be needed to execute the agreements; without insurance, the estates or shareholders might have to sell assets and/or go into debt to assure continuance of the businesses.

THE PERSONAL SIDE OF ESTATE PLANNING

A common goal in estate planning is to conserve personal assets when death occurs after retirement. Many financially secure retirees will usually want to pass on as much of their wealth as possible to the next generation.

If you have taken a lifetime to build a portfolio of investment and personal assets, it is only prudent to consider the next course of action: the development of a plan to conserve the estate. You have already created a plan that will leave you financially comfortable for the rest of your life, incorporating a strategy for continued income indexed to inflation. It's time for the next step.

Personal assets may include real estate (e.g., your home, a cottage or other vacation property and/or rental property); RRSP and RRIF assets; your unregistered (non-RRSP) portfolio; liquid assets, such as cash; term deposits; guaranteed investment certificates (GICs); collectibles and other valuables, such as antiques, art and jewellery.

There are several factors—sometimes challenges—to consider when planning to transfer assets to loved ones at death. All of these are solvable with proper advance planning. They include:

◆   time delays
◆   estate-transfer costs including legal, probate and administration fees, and taxes
◆   confusion about the intent or the instruction of the deceased
◆   inappropriate naming of estate executors or trustees

Time delays

Well-structured estate transfers may take as little as one to six months to complete. Poorly structured ones may require many years. The longer it takes, the more expensive the transfer process generally is, and the more frustrated the beneficiaries may become.

There are several ways to expedite the process. These include:

- ♦ having a well-conceived last will and testament (on paper)
- ♦ using competent, preferably experienced executors or estate trustees
- ♦ passing along as many assets as possible *outside* the will so they won't be held up by probate. It helps to use named beneficiary arrangements that are available with life-insurance company GICs and with segregated (mutual) funds.
- ♦ keeping enough liquid cash handy to pay estate costs promptly

Estate transfer costs

Many people are surprised (to say nothing about horrified) when they see how much the value of an estate can become diminished. Erosion often occurs because of:

♦ **Legal fees.** It is well worth paying for good legal and accounting advice. These professionals are well trained, competent individuals with high standards of ethical conduct. However, their services cost money. The more work an estate requires, the higher the legal and accounting bills will be. Legal fees may range from 1.5% to 8% of an estate's value. If the transfer is clear and simple, the cost could be in the 1.5% range. If it's convoluted, ill prepared and murky, the bill could be as much as 8%. This translates to $1,500 through $8,000 to settle a $100,000 estate.

♦ **Probate.** This fee could be from 0.5% to 1.5 % of the value of the estate. It's a provincial fee so the amount depends upon where the will is probated.

♦ **Administration and estate-transfer fees.** These can amount to as much as 3% of the estate. If a family member is executor or trustee, there may be no fee. But if a trustee has to take time off work to do the job, or incurs incidental expenses such as gas, long-distance telephone, etc., these are usually charged to the estate.

♦ **Tax.** An estate could be in for a substantial tax bill, especially if there are:

♦   unrealized capital gains in an unregistered (non-RRSP or non-RRIF) portfolio

♦   RRSP or RRIF portfolios bequeathed to an individual other than a spouse, dependent child or grandchild

♦   deemed dispositions of a property or business. At death all the deceased's assets are deemed disposed of (as if they were sold), unless going to a spouse. Tax liability could be as much as half the value of the asset itself.

Solutions

There are some practical solutions to these potential problems:

♦   Pass assets directly to named beneficiaries where possible. You could do this by transferring the asset before death. In the case of a home, this might be changing ownership to joint tenancy with rights of survivorship. This could avoid legal, probate and administrative costs at death. It could also avoid some of the costs of tax on a deemed disposition. However, you may be tapped for some income tax at the time of ownership transfer. Definitely check with your accountant before attempting this. In general, tax payable while you're still alive if you transfer ownership is much less than transferring after death.

♦   Use life insurance to fund the cost of tax or fees at death. One of the most overlooked, simplest and elegant solutions is to have an adequate amount of permanent estate life insurance for this purpose. The cost of life insurance premiums for the appropriate amount of coverage when you are alive is a lot less than it would cost your heirs if the estate were left to cover its own expenses.

With this approach, you could set up the asset that will cause the tax problem, so it would provide the money to pay the life insurance premiums. This is especially true in the case of assets like your unregistered portfolio and also RRSPs and RRIFs. For example, you own a RRIF that earns 10%. Instead of withdrawing that 10% as income, take only 8% to spend. You could use the 2% balance to pay the insurance premium. A $100,000 RRIF could provide $1,000 to $2,000 (after tax) towards premium cost. Your death triggers the tax liability but the insurance proceeds trigger the financial solution: a tax-free death benefit that offsets the tax and leaves the asset intact for beneficiaries.

Confusion with respect to intent

Some estates are more costly to settle because the will, if there is one, is unclear about whom is to inherit which asset. This often happens in the case of second marriages or families, or where the deceased intended to leave a cash bequest to beneficiaries other than the current or immediate family. Sometimes the deceased even specified a certain amount to go to certain individuals, but there is no cash available to do it.

Life insurance can help here, too. These are a couple of hypothetical examples (that could easily happen), where potential problems could damage the estate values—and the relationships among the surviving family members:

Example number One

The Smiths had divorced several years ago and George remarried. He has two sons from the first marriage and a thriving manufacturing business worth $2 million. He also has $200,000 in RRSPs, $400,000 in cash and a house worth $500,000. There are no financial obligations to his first wife, who is still living—she had already received her settlement. George wants to leave most of his assets to his sons, but also wants to provide for his second wife, who cannot support herself financially. His only debt is a $200,000 mortgage on the house. His will specifies that all assets go to his two sons, equally. If George should die without making changes, there are problems:

♦ His RRSP, which goes to his sons rather than his second wife, will be hit with about $100,000 in taxes.

♦ The home is supposed to go to his sons, but the second wife could contest this instruction since it is her matrimonial home (even if it is in George's name alone). Besides, he doesn't want to leave her without a place to live.

♦ His business will be assessed a deemed-disposition tax by Revenue Canada. That means any growth beyond the recognized $500,000 tax-free capital gains allowance will be subject to tax in his estate. The actual amount could be as much as $750,000.

♦ If the sons get the $400,000 cash, George's second wife will undoubtedly be destitute.

Solutions

George should consider these changes:

♦ put the house jointly in his own name and his wife's, and insure the $200,000 mortgage on his life and hers
♦ leave the RRSPs to his wife, thus avoiding income tax
♦ divide the cash among his second wife and two sons, in some appropriate fashion
♦ buy life insurance to cover the business estate taxes. It could be relatively low-cost term insurance for now
♦ buy life insurance to offset the value of the house, cash and RRSPs he is leaving to his second wife (about $600,000 in total) and designate his sons as beneficiaries

Example number two

Harry Jones' wife died, and he later remarried. He has one adult daughter from the first marriage, but no children from the second. His second wife has three adult children from her first marriage. Harry's will stipulates in one place that the house should go to his second wife. In another place he has it going to his daughter. His second wife has adequate pension income of her own as long as she could stay in a house that is paid for. If he dies with this ambiguous will, his daughter and second wife could end up in court.

The solution is for Harry to ask his lawyer to redraft the will to clarify who gets the house. If he wants his wife to have it, he should leave it to her. To even things up, he could buy life insurance in favour of his daughter. Alternatively, he could leave the house to the daughter, with a life interest to his second wife so she could live there as long as she wanted to. He should have life insurance payable to the estate in this case, to maintain the house for the second wife until her death, at which time the daughter would inherit.

To summarize

If you have accumulated any assets worth listing, you should be clear where you want them to go when you die. With a little forethought and good management, you can make sure everything is transferred to the right people in reasonable time at the least cost. Your personal financial planner can help and so can your lawyer and accountant. Don't be afraid to use them.

LISE ALLIN is president of Money Concepts, Belleville, and regional vice-president, with Richard, of Money Concepts (Upper Canada region). She graduated from Queen's University with a B.Sc. and has a master's degree in Public Administration. She administers more than $100 million in client assets.

Lise handles most aspects of personal financial planning, though she tends to focus on corporate planning, pension consulting, implementation and windup, asset management, RRIFs, annuities and RRSPs, severance planning and investments, estate planning and business insurance, charitable bequest insurance and portfolio management.

She has been actively involved in the Kingston/Belleville community, and has been founding director of a number of organizations. Currently she is a member of the board of governors of Kingston General Hospital.

RICHARD KIZELL is president of Money Concepts in Kingston, Ontario, and partner with Lise of a Money Concepts regional business in southeastern Ontario. He started his Money Concepts office in 1986 and joined forces with Lise in 1987. They now operate six offices in the area.

Richard graduated from Queen's University with a BA in political science and history in 1977. He has earned his CLU, RFP and CFP since joining Money Concepts.

He is very active in community affairs. At the time of writing he is co-chair of a committee for the City of Kingston to build a new convention, performing arts centre and arena. He is a member of the Downtown Kingston Economic Development Committee, a former board member of the Greater Kingston Chamber of Commerce, finance chair of the Beth Israel Congregation and chair of the United Israel Appeal Campaign for Kingston. He is also treasurer of B'nai Brith Lodge 1191 Kingston and chair of the Annual B'nai Brith Kingston Millionaires Night.

Richard is married to Cheryl and they have two teenaged girls, Valerie and Erin. When not working, Richard enjoys boating, skiing, travelling, hiking and the theatre.

Richard may be reached in Kingston by telephone at 613-548-3031 and by fax at 613-548-7306.

Lise may be reached in Belleville by telephone at 613-968-6751 and by fax at 613-968-2845.

9

Six Steps to Building a Bigger Estate

You borrow money;
Insure your life;
Withdraw RRSP funds;
And all the time minimize tax.

By Carol Clements, CFP
& Signy Lawson, MBA

*D*espite governments' constant efforts to enhance their income at taxpayers' expense, there are still some creative ways to maximize your estate and leave as much as possible to your heirs. This is of interest to everybody, but especially to business owners and individuals with significant investment assets and cottages. You are not limited just to RRSPs if you want to shelter investment income to create a larger estate, or if you need more retirement income for yourself.

Many investors could profit from the techniques we will describe, but those who might benefit the most, are likely to:

- have excess cash flow that they are placing in non-RRSP investments
- be comfortable with the ups and down of equity investments
- have sufficient financial resources so they don't need to draw on their RRSPs for income
- have a need for permanent life insurance
- want to pass on an estate as large as possible to the next generation
- would like to be philanthropic either at death or during their lifetime

There is risk associated with the strategy we outline, but with the aid of an astute financial planner, you should be able to minimize risk, or at least manage it confidently.

Tax-free RRSP withdrawals?

We are suggesting a complex, multi-step process, so you might have to read this chapter several times before you grasp all the elements fully. As you read, remember the objective is to save yourself tax, enhance your retirement income (if needed) and maximize the value of your estate for your heirs. The concept of withdrawing money from your RRSP tax free is a key element in the process.

Here's a quick summary of the steps involved:

1.   Secure a loan on the basis of making periodic payments to consist of interest only.

2.   Invest the borrowed money in equity mutual funds.

3.   Make modest RRSP withdrawals to cover the loan-interest cost.

The next 3 steps are optional, and can be done individually or in combination:

4.   Buy permanent life insurance—a universal life policy that meets your particular needs.

5.   Assign the life insurance policy to a financial institution as collateral for an annual loan you will take over a period of years. Like a reverse mortgage, you won't make any repayment and the interest will accumulate. Eventually the life insurance proceeds will repay the loan and accumulated interest, upon your death.

6.   Redeem 10% from some of your mutual funds each year to pay the insurance premiums.

Let's expand on these steps

First, we set the scene. You and your spouse are ages 60 and 62, healthy and retired. Your two children in their early 30s are married and live in their own homes. You have a net worth of $1,200,000. It consists of RRSPs worth $500,000, other investments of $500,000 plus a $200,000 home. One of you draws a $60,000 annual pension and the other $10,000. For the most part, this income is sufficient for your lifestyle. Your wills direct that at the death of the last spouse, the children shall share your estate equally. In the meantime, you prefer to keep control of your assets because you would like your children to provide for themselves during your lifetime. Besides, if you or your spouse should fall seriously ill, you never know how much money you may need for adequate health care.

Please note that premium costs or interest rates we use are rough estimates and for illustrative purposes only.

STEP ONE

You are conservative so you are comfortable borrowing $100,000—only 10% of your net worth not including the house value. Using your house as collateral, you take out a loan, with payments to be interest only. You must be in a financial position to comfortably handle the interest payments. Since you are securing this line of credit with collateral, you should be able to negotiate a lending rate at bank prime: let's assume 7%. That translates into an annual interest expense of $7,000, which is a tax-deductible item since you have used the loan for investment purposes.

STEP TWO

You use the $100,000 loan to buy one or more good quality, equity mutual funds. Use mutual funds because they allow *Step Six* to work more easily, as you will see. Another reason to use mutual funds is that they may grow with minimal annual tax ramifications: most of their growth should be in the form of capital gains, taxable usually only when you sell.

STEP THREE

To pay the interest cost from *Step One*, you redeem $7,000 each year from your RRSP. The financial institution that holds your RRSP is obligated to withhold 10% to 30% against tax upon withdrawal (10% on withdrawals less than $5,000; 20% if it is between $5,000 and $15,000; and 30% if you withdraw more than $15,000). You will get a refund for this when you file your tax return at the end of the year. The RRSP withdrawal is considered taxable income but the $7,000 loan-interest expense is tax deductible, so the cost of one nullifies the cost of the other.

Congratulations. You have successfully taken money from your RRSP without adding to your personal income tax. In the meantime your $100,000 in mutual funds continues to gain in value. Eat your heart out, tax department.

At a later date, the bank (or whomever you borrowed the money from) will have its loan repaid when the investment is sold. In the meantime you expect to have made money on the original investment. Because stock markets and investment values fluctuate, it is essential that you view this strategy as moderately long term (five years at least). You must be comfortable living with the ups and downs of fund values, and not panic and sell. Especially don't sell if your investment falls below the original $100,000. That is one sure way to turn this into a losing proposition.

Remember: it's best to be conservative in your approach to money management. We recommend that you borrow no more than 10% to 20% of your net worth.

Optional steps

The steps and strategies from here on are optional, but if tax is likely to play an unwelcome role at time of death, they can be useful pieces to fill in the retirement and estate-planning puzzle. You are looking at a time horizon of at least 10 years to retirement. On the one hand, you may want to enhance your retirement income so you have to build a bigger retirement nest egg. On the other, you may wish to leave a larger estate to your heirs.

Since the government has eliminated most other tax shelters, the approach we recommend has been gaining a great deal of attention from investors. In fact, some insurance companies are specifically designing insurance products that maximize the investment benefits and minimize the life insurance portion—a key constituent of this approach.

STEP FOUR

You buy a $250,000 universal life insurance policy that pays out upon the death of the second spouse (joint, last-to-die). The annual premium cost is $6,000. You may contribute additional amounts to the investment portion of the policy up to an annual maximum (about $10,000 per year in our example).

Universal is a form of permanent life insurance that combines term insurance coverage with an investment component. We suggest universal rather than whole life since universal allows you to select and monitor the investment component. You can use guaranteed investment certificates (GICs) or stock-market indexed funds.

This approach is the next best tax shelter to RRSPs because all the investment growth is tax-deferred just like an RRSP. Over time your investment should grow significantly greater than by simply investing the money outside a shelter and paying tax annually on the return. You will need to allow approximately 10 years for the tax-deferred compounding to become beneficial, before you withdraw from it.

When you take money from the policy's investment component, there are tax consequences. You pay tax on the amount withdrawn less the "adjusted cost base" of the policy (the ACB is the mortality cost or cost of the insurance component). The amount varies depending on your age and the age of the policy.

Step Four helps you create additional retirement income above and beyond your RRSPs. It takes advantage of tax-free compounding along the way. Is there a way to get a hold of this money without further tax consequence? Perhaps. Read on through *Step Five*.

STEP FIVE

You approach your friendly banker for an annual loan over a period of five to 10 years (longer if the numbers can justify it). As collateral you assign the investment portion of your insurance policy to the bank. You make no annual principal or interest repayments; it works much like a reverse mortgage, compounding the interest cost over time. You use the loan proceeds for income. Because it is a loan, there is no tax payable on this income stream. The accumulating and compounding interest charges must grow at a lesser rate than the growth in the policy's investment funds over the five to 10 years—or the investments in the policy will become exhausted by the loan liability and the policy would terminate.

When you die, the loans are paid off through the assignment of the insurance policy's investment pool. Proceeds from the policy are tax free, so you have just created more retirement income without tax consequences. Don't forget, in addition to the loan payoff, the insurance company pays out the face value of the policy itself, tax free, to your named beneficiaries.

STEP SIX

How do you pay for the life insurance in *Step Five*? In *Step One*, you invested $100,000 in an equity mutual fund. Over the period of the annual loan, you redeem 10% of the fund or funds every year to pay the insurance premiums. Historically, the performance in equities over the long term has been greater than 10% so this should not jeopardize the repayment of the *Step-One* loan that you took out.

There is one thing to be careful of: Revenue Canada is always concerned about tax avoidance. If sometime down the road it changes the regulations and decides that you have taken these steps primarily to avoid tax, you will have created additional retirement income all right, but you might incur some tax liabilities. But then again, you might not. It should be noted that in the past when Revenue Canada has made changes, they have grandfathered existing policies. This means old rules apply to existing policies and they are unaffected by legislation changes.

If you had been fortunate enough not to need the money that has compounded tax free, when you die your beneficiaries will get it all tax free (unlike with an RRSP)! Hallelujah! It's a great estate-planning tool.

If at any time you need some of the money you have invested in the insurance policy to bolster your income or to cover unexpected healthcare costs, you could use some of the investment portion of the policy not needed to support the loan collateral or cost of insurance.

There are risks

Investing and tax-planning strategies always contain an element of risk. Consider these:

♦ Your borrowing costs exceed the rate of return you average from your investments.

♦ Revenue Canada changes legislation and does not grandfather existing policies.

♦ There is a significant downturn in the equity markets and you panic and sell your investments at a lower price than the value of the loan.

♦ Your financial planner dies and you can't remember why you did all of this!

You minimize risks by using the expertise of a competent planner, especially one from a large and well-established organization that provides continuity.

CAROL CLEMENTS and SIGNY LAWSON are joint owners of the Money Concepts Financial Planning Centre in Stouffville, Ontario. Colleagues describe them as dynamic businesswomen who thoroughly enjoy all aspects of their lives, business and personal. It's apparent that they love what they are doing.

Carol, a BA and BSW graduate of McMaster University, joined the investment industry in 1987 as a stockbroker. Signy, an MBA graduate of the University of Saskatchewan, worked as a management consultant with one of the major accounting firms prior to starting the Money Concepts business in 1991.

Their entrepreneurial spirit has fueled the growth of their successful business with millions of dollars under administration and the creation of many effective estate plans for clients. One of their greatest professional rewards is that they can educate and advise business owners and self-employed professionals to prudently manage their financial affairs and achieve their goals. They value their role as financial planners because it is a continuing learning process that keeps them mentally stimulated. They relish the close and special relationships they develop with clients, which adds joy to their lives.

Signy and Carol can't imagine having a better business relationship. They credit their country roots and similar values for making the partnership an effortless one. They recognize that life has been good to them and they do what they can to give something back through involvement in local charities and business organizations.

Carol describes as her best personal accomplishment her marriage to her husband, Doug. They enjoy romping on their country property with their two black Labrador retrievers, Henry and Hughie. Carol is a fitness fan and has completed many marathon races. You also may find her training horses at the family farm.

When Signy isn't working, she loves to golf, garden, swim and attend theatre and arts events. She and husband, Doug, spend many a summer evening poolside with their two teenage children.

Carol and Signy may be reached in Stouffville by telephone 905-642-4540 and by fax at 905-642-4537. Their e-mail address is mconstf@interlog.com.

10

Risk Management, Simplified

By Charles Zwicker, P.Eng, MBA, RFP
& Jocelyn MacKenzie, CGA, CFP, RFP

*R*isk management is an area of financial planning that is often overlooked or not thoroughly addressed. It involves a planner's assessment of whether an individual or family has life, disability, critical illness, property and/or liability insurance, and whether it is the right type and amount of coverage to meet their particular needs.

Property and liability insurance protects us against damage or loss of vehicles, home, jewellery, artworks and some accidents. Life insurance replaces the income of one or more breadwinners who die prematurely. Disability insurance replaces a portion of earned income when you are disabled by accident or illness and cannot work for a period of time. It will probably cover only everyday living costs. For perspective, here is a list of everyday basic living expenses for a family of four:

	Monthly
Retirement savings (10% of income)	$500
Education savings for two children	230
Food	400
Housing (rent, mortgage, utilities, taxes)	1,100
Clothing	200
Transportation (buy/lease, maintenance)	450
Entertainment, sports/hobbies, vacation	500
TOTAL	**$3,380**

Over 20 years this amounts to $1,122,558, assuming inflation at 3% per year.

Planners do not look at insurance in isolation. They have to consider whether, given limited financial resources, a client should carry the necessary amount of insurance or instead maximize RRSPs or pay down a mortgage quickly. In many cases financial planning means making choices.

Disability insurance is covered in another chapter so we won't deal with it. Nor will we discuss property or liability coverage since they are relatively commonplace and straightforward. Keep in mind that wherever we mention insurance costs, they are actual quotes from various carriers at the time of writing. They are derived from a common insurance-industry software program called Lifeguide, which has access to the premiums of many companies. Needless to say, the names illustrating our examples are fictitious.

LIFE INSURANCE: THE OLD AND THE NEW

There are two main types of life insurance: term and permanent. Term provides protection only for a specific period of time or to a particular age. Permanent insurance is in force until death and it may combine insurance with a pool of investments used to help fund the policy.

When you compare policies, the factors to consider are the face amount (death benefit), the premium (cost of the insurance) and the structure (riders, dividends and pools of investments). This last item comes only with permanent types of insurance and it makes them much more difficult to assess than term policies. A general rule often used within the industry to assess, in general, the amount of insurance needed, is 10 times income or 7.5 times income if you have no debt.

Term can be the cheapest

Term is the least expensive form of insurance and the most commonly used. It is, in essence, a temporary insurance often used for a single purpose, such as paying off debts or providing a lump sum of capital to replace loss of income. It can be attractive for a young family on a modest budget.

The yearly premium for term insurance is guaranteed not to increase for a defined period of time. A common example is a Term 10 Renewable and Convertible policy. Term 10 means that the annual premiums remain unchanged for 10 years. The renewable option means that after 10 years the policy may be renewed for another 10-year term but at a new rate based on your current age, for a predetermined amount set out in the initial contract. The renewal premium is often twice as much or more than the old one. You may include other options such as joint lives (spouses, family members or business associates), or a rider that pays the premiums in the event of disability.

Convertible means that you may convert or exchange the policy at any time (so long as it is in good standing) to another type of insurance with the same company, without further evidence of insurability. The amount of new coverage, known as "face value," cannot exceed the amount of the contract being converted. You might, for example, convert a policy if you need longer-term coverage perhaps with level premiums. You might suffer an illness that would make you uninsurable so you switch from a term policy to permanent coverage that has a savings element within it.

You may obtain term insurance from organizations such as alumni or professional associations and employers. These are typically annual, renewable, term policies and every year the premium will go up according to your age. The premiums can be inexpensive but you do not have much control. For instance, the carrier could change or even cancel coverage at any time, especially if you change jobs. Also, when you reach a certain age, usually 60 or 65, the coverage may automatically shrink or cease.

An example of term-insurance costs

A young woman with children and who is a partner in a small business requires term insurance coverage for different needs. As a mother she must leave enough money, should she die prematurely, to replace her income until the children are educated and have become independent. Her business, if she died, would need a lump sum to provide financial stability plus funds to hire someone to replace her. Her business partner would need coverage to provide a lump-sum payment that would allow him to buy her share of the business from her family. Each of these situations requires coverage for different lengths of time. Here is about what it would cost for a $500,000 term policy, assuming she is 37, a non-smoker and has no medical rating:

ANNUAL PREMIUM	10 YEARS	20 YEARS	TO AGE 65
Years 1 to 10	$480	$707	$1,118
Years 11 to 20	1,680	707	1,118
Years 21 to 28	4,200	5,820	1,118
Total paid by age 65	$55,200	$60,700	$31,304

The most appropriate policy for anyone depends upon its purpose, the length of time it's required and the resources available to pay the premiums.

Permanent insurance is more complicated than term

Permanent insurance, which includes whole life, term-to-100 and universal life (UL), has more features than term, and is suitable in more circumstances. Among these is the need for insurance after retirement—critical for families who depend heavily on employer pensions for income. The surviving spouse of a pensioner is often forced to live on 50% of the pension and sometimes even less. This is a devastating position to be in. At a time of grief and major adjustments, financial concerns can be overwhelming for the family. Do not ignore the need for adequate life insurance after retirement.

Whole life is an older type of coverage

This is not used much these days. It derives its name from the fact that it protects the buyer for his/her whole (entire) life. Premiums remain the same amount throughout the life of most whole-life policies. Because of this levelling out, it can appear more expensive than term insurance during the earlier years. Partly offsetting this are guarantees by the insurance company of a cash-surrender value. You might decide to cancel the policy and stop paying premiums. In that case you would be able to obtain a refund of whatever the policy has built up in cash value. These higher early premiums also can allow insurance companies to include a number of ancillary benefits, among them automatic premium loans, extended term insurance and paid-up insurance. This last item protects policyholders from cancellation if they can't pay the premiums for a while.

The industry also offers "participating" whole-life policies. This means policyholders participate in the profits of the insurance company and receive dividends or distributions that would add to policy reserves, death benefits and/or cash value. The insured might opt, after a time, to have these reserves and dividends cover the cost of the premiums for the balance of the contract. In recent years this has become controversial because earnings have not been as high as projected at the time of sale and as a result the policyholder must pay premiums longer than originally expected.

Whole-life policies did not completely satisfy many buyers for two reasons:

1.   Many did not want to fund a cash value that they would not claim.

2.   The reserve was owned and controlled by the insurance company and the policyholder had no say in how it was invested. Often, returns were less than a policyholder could earn from other investments.

Term-to-100 and universal life are newer solutions

The life insurance industry responded to the less-than-satisfactory whole-life situation with two different policies: term-to-100 and universal life. **Term-to-100** insurance does not have a cash-surrender value, and the premium stays the same until the holder reaches age 100, when the policy becomes paid up. **Universal life** is a term policy combined with an investment fund. That sounds like whole life and it is, with one big difference: the investment portion of the coverage is separate and the policyholder determines the investments. These accumulate free of tax. This new flexibility means that the owner decides:

♦   the amount to go into the investment fund (within prescribed limits)
♦   the amount of insurance coverage, by increasing or decreasing the insurance component of the policy
♦   the amount and duration of premiums
♦   the types of investments in the fund
♦   whether to withdraw amounts from the fund, and when

The UL policy may cover a single life or more. For example, insurance for estate-preservation purposes is often issued jointly on two spouses, with the insurance paying out upon the death of the second spouse. This delays the insurance payout so premiums are significantly lower than they would be for single coverage. You may choose to pay premiums until the death of either the first spouse or the second spouse (they are lower in the former case) or for a specific period of time (e.g., five or 10 years) or all at once in a lump sum.

Term-to-100 premiums are much lower than for UL, but are payable for life. On the next page is a comparison of the two: $200,000 coverage for a woman age 58 and her husband, 65. Both are in good health and the type of coverage is joint-last-to-die:

TYPE		_PREMIUM_
◆ Term-to-100		$1,949/yr 'til second spouse dies
◆ Universal Life		
	◆ Paid up after five years	$7,000/year
	◆ Paid up after 10 years	$4,000/year

In each case, the face amount of $200,000 is payable upon the death of the second spouse, even if that happens within a year of taking out the policy. Some people like the T100 policy because of the lower premiums for a given amount of coverage. If, however, you prefer to have the policy paid up as soon as possible so you do not have to continue making payments, UL might be your choice. Also, UL is more flexible, since you may modify the insurance coverage to suit changing needs over time. It also allows a tax-free asset build-up in its separate investment fund. Costs are typical at time of writing.

Both term-to-100 and universal life are useful for estate preservation, although UL can have other purposes. For instance, it is useful for the dual purpose of providing low-cost life insurance for children and to fund their education. The investment amount grows tax free and the child takes it when required for school fees. The child may later on decide to augment the insurance coverage by contributing to the investment fund.

Withdraw funds tax free by leveraging

A policyholder may withdraw money from the investment fund of a UL policy at any time (perhaps to supplement retirement income), but normally it is taxable as income (though the policy beneficiary will get it tax free upon the death of the policy owner). There is a way for an owner to get money out without tax liability, however. It is called _leveraged life insurance._ You arrange for a bank loan using the investment fund as collateral. The principal and interest accumulate during the life of the policyholder and is paid off with tax-free insurance proceeds upon the policyholder's death.

Good for estate planning, too

These policies are ideal for estate planning. Assets usually pass tax-free to a surviving spouse, but are deemed to have been disposed of upon the death of the survivor. This creates a tax liability that could be significant—e.g., about 50% of RRSP and/or RRIF amounts—since the disposition is added to that year's other income.

Here's an illustration of life insurance used for estate preservation; Mary's spouse pre-deceased her:

ASSETS	AMOUNT	CAPITAL GAIN	TAX LIABILITY AFTER DEATH	COMMENT
RRIF	$300,000	$0	$150,000	50% tax
INVESTMENTS	250,000	100,000	37,500	75% cap. gain @ 50%
COTTAGE	150,000	50,000	18,000	75% cap. gain @ 50%
House	200,000	0	0	No tax (principal res.)
TOTAL			**$205,500**	

If Mary were to have life insurance of $205,000 when she dies, that could cover the tax and the entire estate could go to her beneficiaries. It also means the executors do not have to sell assets to pay tax at a time when the stock or real estate markets might be at a low ebb.

Permanent insurance can provide growth to offset tax

Here's an example of how permanent insurance can help offset tax liability later in life so a couple can leave a maximum amount to their children. Sam and Evelyn are 48, live in a mortgage-free home, have RRSPs and an investment portfolio in Evelyn's name and they own a cottage. They crystallized the cottage capital gains in 1994 at $125,000. Sam earns $75,000 and Evelyn $100,000, annually. They still have about $25,000 every year after RRSP contributions, which they would like to invest. They are concerned about the income taxes they will have to pay as these investments grow over the years.

The table (next page) is a snapshot of the expected income-tax liability if both spouses were to die next week, perhaps in a car accident, and at age 70.

We are assuming growth rates of 3% annually for home and cottage, and 10% for RRSPs and investments. There would be no tax on the sale of a principal residence and only 75% of investment capital gains are taxable (at the top marginal tax rate of about 50%).

Either a UL or term-to-100 policy of $150,000 would provide for their immediate needs. Only the UL policy, however, would grow to match their future needs, especially at age 70. So they chose a UL policy since it allowed them to increase coverage to suit their changing needs.

Asset	Current Value	Current Tax Liability	Estimated Value at Age 70	Estimated Tax Liability at Age 70
Home	$200,000	$0	$383,000	$0
RRSPs	250,000	125,0000	2,035,000	1,017,000
Cottage	125,000	0	239,000	43,000
Investments	100,000	0	815,000	268,000
TOTAL		$125,000		$1,328,000

A $500,000 universal policy with maximum annual contributions would cost them about $11,500 per year if they pay it up over 10 years ($20,000 for a faster five-year paid-up period). At age 70 the policy should be worth about $770,000, assuming the investment portion grew at an average rate of 6% annually ($890,000 at a growth rate of 8%). This would still leave about a $400,000 tax liability assuming 8% investment growth. If they were to make annual deposits to the policy beyond the 10 year premium period, they could expect to cover that gap. For example, at an 8% annual yield, they would have to make annual contributions of about $11,500 for 20 years. The cost is small compared to the benfit: over 20 years, premiums of about $230,000 provide a death benefit of $1.3 million.

The basic message is this: you have worked hard lifelong to accumulate assets. If you want to pass them on to your children or other beneficiaries rather than losing a significant portion to the government in tax, permanent insurance is a good solution. The cost of insurance is small compared to the benefits received, some of which you get as soon as you buy the policy.

CRITICAL ILLNESS INSURANCE: NEW AND ESSENTIAL

Critical illness insurance is a new type of term insurance that pays living policyholders who incur severely debilitating or life-threatening illnesses. You could consider it essential coverage in that we are all living longer and our retirement funds must last much longer. If we are hit by a critical illness, the extra costs involved could severely curtail our standard of living.

Consider these facts:

♦   One in three Canadians will develop some form of life-threatening cancer.

♦   The survival rate after five years for the most common 10 cancers is 50%.

♦   One in four Canadians will contract heart disease.

♦   A new diabetic is diagnosed every 50 seconds in Canada.

♦   More than 300,000 Canadians suffer from Alzheimer's disease.

Critical illness insurance fills in the gap between disability and life insurance. It helps you maintain your lifestyle during and after the illness and pays the additional medical costs, living expenses and possible modifications to your home if you are diagnosed with a critical illness. Critical illness usually includes heart attack, stroke, life-threatening cancer, kidney failure, blindness, deafness, major organ transplant, multiple sclerosis and paralysis. You would receive a lump-sum payment or a combination of lump-sum and regular, periodic payments, tax free, for a specified period of time. Generally the amounts range from $25,000 to $1,000,000.

This is really a form of term insurance, so it will expire or no longer be available to you, typically around age 70—although recently a permanent term-to-100 version of this insurance has been introduced. It is available with different features and can be used for different applications. Premiums can be set so that they remain the same for the length of coverage or increase at 10-year intervals. Cost can be based on individual or joint coverage (family, spouses or business partners).

Critical illness insurance is suitable for individuals and families. It can be included in buy/sell agreements for shareholders. Self-employed individuals can use it to pay off creditors, companies can provide it for key personnel to help compensate for possible loss of customers or it can be an executive perk. Premiums generally are more expensive than for 10-year term insurance but less than disability-income insurance. For example, at the time of writing, cost for $100,000 coverage on a male non-smoker aged 38, would be about $525 per year. For a female it would be about $420.

Why critical illness insurance can be so essential

Debbie, a 32-year-old single mom of two school-age children, is a typical example of why disability insurance alone is not enough. She was diagnosed with breast cancer. Doctors said surgery will remove the tumour but Debbie will also need chemotherapy and radiation.

She has long-term disability coverage that pays 66% of her current $47,000 annual salary, for a maximum period of 24 months. This is non-taxable and we calculate that she has sufficient income for regular living expenses. In hospital, though, little things such as television rental and magazines are additional costs.

Debbie has the surgery and starts treatment; she feels sicker and weaker. Her parents can keep the children some nights, but she has to come up with money for extra after-school day care. She also has to engage a person to look after the house and do the laundry. This costs $100 every week. Home care comes in once or twice a week to help her bathe and do chores—at another $100 per week. Her employer's benefit package covers up to 80% of prescription expense but does not include costs for wigs and hair pieces (she lost her hair during chemo), over-the-counter drugs for frequent nausea or cosmetics to cloak complexion problems.

She has to modify the bathtub to install a bar across it and incurs more costs for taxis to and from treatments. On top of that there are expenses for the children's activities because she is too sick to do things with them herself, and she has to hire a handyman to cut the lawn and handle miscellaneous chores. Add to that the cost of a short, modest holiday with the children before she returns to work.

After the first treatments her blood counts are very low and that delays the next treatment round by a couple of months. Debbie is able to return to work two and a half years after being diagnosed. In the meantime she needed a new wardrobe because she lost so much weight. This is a summary of her *extra* costs, over and above disability payments:

	WEEKLY
Cleaning, *home care & transportation ($250/week)*	$32,500
Kids *activities & day care ($75/week)*	9,750
New *wardrobe*	2,000
Bathroom *modification*	750
Holiday *with children*	2,500
Income *for 6 months after disability coverage ceased*	15,500
TOTAL	**$63,000**

Extra costs add up quickly, even if you have disability insurance. This example is based on a true story and the circumstances were not exceptional. It pays to have critical-illness insurance.

JOCELYN MACKENZIE and CHARLES ZWICKER are partners in a Money Concepts Ottawa, Ontario, office. They have earned their Certified Financial Planner (CFP) and Registered Financial Planner (RFP) designations and combine for more than 35 years' experience in financial planning and business services. Their office includes six other financial planners and support staff who provide bilingual services.

Jocelyn's background before financial planning includes almost a decade with a national accounting firm in the small-business and personal-tax areas and five years in private practice as a professional accountant and tax planner. Her clients include individuals, families and businesses from all walks of life. In recent years she has been focusing especially on people affected by corporate re-organization and downsizing, small business owners/managers/professionals and women.

Jocelyn is mother to three young children and together they enjoy summer camp and sporting activities. Giving back to the community and involvement in the business community are important parts of her life. Recent activities and committee work include: 1997 and 1998 captain of the Money Concepts Ottawa team entered in the MDS Nordion Corporate Challenge supporting the Women's Breast Health Centre; member of the President's Council, Ottawa Civic Hospital Foundation; 2nd Vice-President, Women's Business Network Association of Ottawa; President, Ottawa Chapter, Canadian Association of Financial Planners; Director, Andrew Fleck Child Care Services; and Chair, National Marketing Committee, Money Concepts (Canada).

Charles' extensive private- and public-sector finance and economics background includes helping develop energy policy for the federal government and founding and acting as finance executive for an electronics firm. His business experience in gathering and analyzing information relative to clients' financial goals, and making recommendations about achieving those goals, has been helpful in the personal financial planning service that he has been providing since 1992.

Charles offers those comprehensive planning services to a broad range of clients including small businesses interested in group-benefit plans. He has a special interest in retirement and estate planning and investing, particularly for those aged 40 and beyond.

Charles and wife, Barbara, have a daughter who lives in Cleveland, Ohio, and a son in Ottawa. Charles is active in the community (as a member of the executive of a tennis club and chairman of the Scouts Group Committee) and in his industry (past executive member of the Ottawa Chapter of the Canadian Association of Financial Planners, and a member of the Ottawa Estate Planning Council). Charles and Barbara enjoy cross-country skiing and skating in the winter, tennis and canoeing in summer.

Jocelyn and Charles may be reached by telephone at 613-731-2000 and by fax at 613-521-8021.

11

Financing Education

Don't put off until tomorrow
What you can do today

By Ed MacDermaid
BA, B.Ed, CFP

*I*n our modern-day mania for government financial restraint and budget-balancing, many social issues have been caught in a squeeze–not the least of which is education. Education costs have risen dramatically during the past 20 years and are projected to go even higher. A four-year post-secondary education in 1995-96 cost about $40,000 if you include tuition, rent, books and food. By 2015 the cost is expected to soar to about $68,000. In the past 10 years alone, according to Statistics Canada, the cost of post-secondary education increased an astounding 152%.

So as parents, what do we do? Are there alternatives? How do we ensure our children's access to education at a reasonable cost? Most people choose from among four more-or-less standard approaches:

1. We can wait until the kids begin university and pay as they go: $67,000 after taxes.

2. They can attend and we pay by mortgaging the house. That's $67,000 amortized over 19 years at $7,500 per year: $142,500.

3. We can begin now investing $101 per month for the next 18 years: $21,685.

4. We can put up a lump sum of $10,494 today. Nice if you can afford it.

Which makes most sense to you? If you chose number 3, you're in the majority.

However there is more to education savings than just dollars and cents. Before you run out and start depositing $101 a month into a savings account, consider some alternatives in more detail. As with most investments, the key issue is rate of return after taxes and, in many cases, maximizing certain tax benefits that allow us to do far more than we might have thought. Let's review three investment options that can maximize the money available to fund education expenses:

OPTION ONE:

Registered Education Savings Plans: a possible 20% return

In 1998 the federal government instituted major reforms to registered education savings plan (RESP) rules in an effort to address the escalating cost of education. RESPs as a result are now more attractive and flexible.

RESPs are tax-deferred savings plans for education. A subscriber sets up a plan for one or more beneficiaries and the resulting pool of money grows in a tax-sheltered environment until the beneficiary starts to use the fund to pay for a post-secondary educational—or until the plan is collapsed (the maximum period for an RESP to exist is 25 years). You may contribute a maximum $42,000 per beneficiary lifetime, and annually not more than $4,000. If you do put in more, you are penalized 1% per month of the excess.

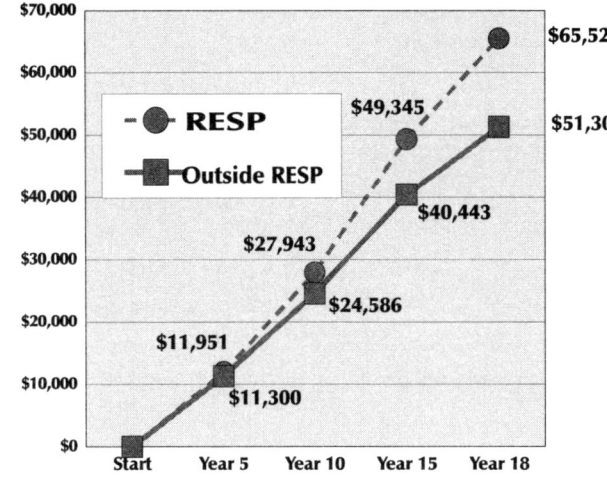

$2,000 annual contribution inside vs. outside RESP
(6% average annual rate of return and a 40% marginal tax rate)

Unlike RRSPs, contributions to an RESP are not tax deductible. But tax on the growth of the plan is deferred. This helps significantly. For example, if you were to deposit $2,000 per year in the form of a guaranteed investment certificate (GIC) yielding 6% annually, the after-tax value of the plan in 18 years would be $51,227. If you placed the $2,000 into an RESP, it would amount to $65,520 after 18 years as the chart on the previous page shows. Since the growth within the plan is taxed in the hands of the recipient, and the recipient as a student will not likely be earning much taxable income, the tax payable could be next to nothing.

What the new, improved RESP does for you

The new RESP rules mean that for every dollar you contribute as a subscriber up to $2,000 per year, the federal government will add 20%, to a maximum of $400 annually or $7,200 lifetime. In other words the $65,520 RESP will become a $78,623 value. To receive this Canada Education Savings Grant (CESG), your child must have a social insurance number (SIN). You get one using an application form available at your local Human Resources Development Canada office. Pretty good so far, and it actually gets better.

You've had the plan, received the CESG $400 each year, and now your child is ready to embark on a journey to higher learning (that does not mean the local cyber cafe). How do you access the money? Here are three ways:

ONE

The government money paid out under an RESP to help a beneficiary attend a post-secondary institution is called Educational Assistance Payments (EAP). The subscriber (you or your spouse or a grandparent, etc.) decides how much the beneficiary should get each year. The subscriber may also choose whether to make the payment from income or capital. Regardless, a certain part of each payment will be attributed to the government's CESG deposits to the plan, based on the ratio of the CESGs to total investment income earned.

Suggestion

You may want to pay out more income from the RESP in the first year if the beneficiary has just graduated from high school and may have had only a couple of months to work in the summer. This could keep the taxable amount down because the student's income likely will be low, and so will the tax (if any). In subsequent years when the student may have worked longer, you could designate less income and more principal—and principal is not taxable.

TWO

Another way to get money from an RESP is a refund of contributions. A subscriber may withdraw all contributions from the plan tax free. If you do, you must repay the CESGs on a pro-rated basis. You must also be wary of withdrawing unassisted contributions (the amount above the $2,000 per year limit). If you take more than $200 of unassisted contributions from the plan, the beneficiaries will not qualify for further CESGs for up to three years.

Suggestion

If you make $4,000 annual RESP contributions, review the situation at the end of 10 years. At this point you withdraw $20,000—your full CESG-assisted payments—without adverse tax consequences. In addition, if you had not used your RRSP contribution limit for several years, you could apply that $20,000 refund as an RRSP catch-up deposit. This would render a portion of your RESP even more tax deductible. If you get to this stage, it's a good idea to seek the advice of a qualified financial planner.

THREE

A third way to withdraw funds is through accumulated income payments. Before the rules changed, if a designated beneficiary did not attend a qualified post-secondary institution, the subscriber could take back the accumulated original contributions and get a note of thanks from a grateful university that had received the investment's earnings. The new RESP rules allow a subscriber to transfer up to $40,000 worth of contributions ($50,000 in 1999) to an RRSP or spousal RRSP if the contribution room is available— and if the plan has been in force for 10 years. If the subscriber does not have enough RRSP contribution room, Revenue Canada taxes the withdrawal as regular income—and adds a 20% penalty. If you are in the 46% tax bracket, your withdrawal could attract a 66% tax. Also, you must collapse the RESP by March 1st of the year following the first accumulated income payment.

Suggestion

If your beneficiary should not opt for higher education, you will be forced into some creative planning. For example, let's suppose all is going well but the apple of your eye announces on high school graduation day, "I've decided to become an existentialist and I'll be leaving for Tibet as soon as I can acquire a good yak." Not only do you stand to lose a treasured apple but you might also lose most of the growth from the RESP investments. Unless, that is, you have taken the following steps: you have made sure your spouse is also a (joint) subscriber on the RESP documentation. This entitles your spouse to half the plan's withdrawn earnings, and depending on his or her income, the tax bite may be less. Capital withdrawals are not affected by tax.

Also, because you have more than one child, you have specified multiple beneficiaries. If one of them does not qualify for EAPs, the remaining children may share the RESP, with the caveat that a maximum of $7,200 worth of CESGs are allowed to each qualifier. If you had four beneficiaries and only three attended university, you would have to repay up to $7,200 to the government.

Not all RESPs are created equal

Based on this thumbnail sketch of RESPs you no doubt have concluded that, in addition to being a tremendous make-work project for civil servants, they are also a great way to provide money for your children's education.

Before you rush right out and set up an RESP, be aware not all of them are created equal. Currently there are two main types: scholarship trusts and mutual-fund RESPs. At this writing, scholarship trusts are somewhat disadvantaged, particularly when it comes to options for winding up the plan. In a mutual-fund RESP, the subscriber controls the amount of payout; in the scholarship trust, the trust decides. As well, in terms of multiple beneficiaries and joint subscribers, mutual funds appear, at this point, to be much more flexible. Finally, as with any investment, there is the question of rate of return. With scholarship trusts, the trusts make all investment decisions, usually subscribing only to guaranteed-investment vehicles (GICs, for example). Mind you, beneficiaries of scholarship trusts often get a break because not every registrant opts for post-secondary education. This means a qualifier may get more than what was projected because the investment-pool growth for any given year may be divided up among fewer beneficiaries than started the plan.

Choose your own investments

Subscribers to an RESP mutual fund may choose their investment vehicle, and its growth dictates how much money the beneficiary eventually gets. Because RESPs are usually long-term investments, they are particularly suitable for long-term investment vehicles, such as international equity-based mutual funds. Over the long term, while international equity funds can be volatile, their rates of return historically have been greater than any guaranteed performer. For example, and I must emphasize the word example, if you had started a mutual-fund RESP in 1980 with the Templeton Growth Fund, your $2,000 annual contribution plus the 20% CESG would be worth approximately $200,000 in 1998 (a 16% average annual rate of return). If your offspring are especially grateful, they may even wish to share with their dear old penniless parents some of the largesse left after education expenses. Or they may be wise enough not only to pay for their education but also to reinvest what's left over or use the money to get started in life.

No phone purchases

A final note of caution: don't buy an RESP over the phone. You're not buying a magazine subscription; you are buying into a dream. Purchasing a dream requires a lot more time, consideration and analysis. Because the RESP structure is new, opportunistic salespeople are peddling them on the phone like carpet cleaning and aluminum siding. You must spend time examining the options, determining the type of the education fund required as well as assessing your ability to pay. This does not mean procrastinate—but a little caution today could prevent unpleasant surprises in the future. Make haste, slowly. The long-term benefits arise from proper planning, not short-term emotional gratification because you have just bought an RESP for your child. Like most dreams, realization depends upon perse-verance and commitment.

OPTION TWO:
In-trust accounts

In-trust (the *in* stands for informal) accounts are plans set up for the benefit of a beneficiary. A formal trust set up by accountants (yikes!) and lawyers (ouch!) can be very expensive. As such, you should use them only when a considerable amount of money is involved since a good accountant and lawyer can be worth their weight in the gold it will cost to set the plan up. Formal trusts are generally used for more than just an education fund. If you don't have the resources, or don't want the hassle of a formal trust, the answer for your child's education may be an informal trust.

When you set up an informal trust, you, the settler, provide the where-withal that is invested for the benefit of the beneficiary. To be legal, there must be intention on the part of the contributor to create a trust. You must clearly describe the investment and beneficiaries involved and name them specifically. In addition, the settler (contributor), cannot be the same person as the trustee who makes the investment decisions in the best interest of the beneficiary. The money held in trust belongs to the beneficiary unequivocally. You as the settler have *given* the property to the trust.

So if you wish to go this route, be sure that apart from the investment contract there is written documentation demonstrating your intention to set up a trust. You must also be clear in writing that the donor is not the trustee and that only the donor contributes and only the trustee withdraws funds. Ultimately, how the funds are used (for the benefit of the beneficiary only) will determine whether the trust could withstand a challenge by Revenue Canada or civil legal action.

In-trust payouts can be multipurpose

Suppose, for a moment, that you have created a legal in-trust to fund your children's education or create an opportunity fund for them. The beauty of the in-trust account is that the trustee can use the money for any purpose that is beneficial to the children (or child). The kids might use it for a European tour, a round-the-world cruise or to pay for those dreaded but ubiquitous dental-retention devices. (These now seem to be required for every child who has teeth.)

An advantage of this type of trust is that capital gains earned by its investments are taxable in the hands of the beneficiary and thus are tax deferred for a number of years. An in-trust account is very flexible in terms of investment options and there are no limits to contributions.

When your child starts at a post-secondary institution, the trustee may use trust money for education costs. If the child does not attend university, he or she could use the money for some other purpose—perhaps a one-way ticket to Seoul to teach English—or learn Korean. When your child or children reach age 21, the informal trust dies and the proceeds become their property.

Informal trusts are an excellent way for grandparents to help grandchildren. An in-trust gift provides the child with investment money now, forces the trustee to use the money for the child's benefit and provides an effective form of income splitting.

Most mutual fund companies will happily set up this type of account. Since interest and dividends earned in the trust are attributable to the donor, it's a good idea to choose investments more heavily capital-gain oriented than dividend- or interest-producing. Most international equity-based mutual funds would suit this purpose.

Better to think than switch

If you have an informal trust now and you are envious of the new RESP plans, don't be too hasty cashing out your trust and switching. Revenue Canada has indicated it will allow in-trust transfers to RESPs, but there are other factors to consider. One consideration offered by a lawyer friend of mine goes like this: suppose you collapse the in-trust account and channel the funds directly to the new RESP. Your child, who today is the apple of your eye, opts not to go to university, or worse still, opts to take a law degree. Upon discovering that you switched, your novice legal eagle may well decide to sue you on the basis that he or she did not give permission to move the funds and is now suffering hardship because in-trust funds that were previously freely available are now restricted by RESP rules. (Only a lawyer would think that way.) If you like the idea of an RESP, consider leaving the trust as is and start a new RESP. The trust account can always be a backup or an emergency fund for the child's well-being.

OPTION THREE:

Leveraged investments

A third option to fund your child's education is leveraged investment. This is simply a strategy in which you borrow for the express purpose of investing, so all the interest cost of the loan is tax deductible. For example, you borrow $10,000 today and earn 10% on it for 18 years, so the investment would end up worth about $56,000. At a reasonable loan-interest rate of, say, 8%, it would cost you $800 per year. If you are in the 46% marginal tax bracket, your net cost would be about $432 per year, or $36 per month. You would save $368 annually and if you used that saving to make an RRSP contribution, you would save a further $165.

Do this for 18 years and your $368 RRSP tax saving (assuming a 10% return) would be worth $18,458. Furthermore, if you reinvest the $165 annual RRSP tax saving at 10%, it would be worth $7,523–nearly enough to pay off the original $10,000 debt.

In 18 years you would have $56,000 in your education-investment account, $18,458 in your RRSP and $7,523 in an open account–all for as little as $36 per month after tax. When you take money from your investments to fund your child's education the income portion becomes taxable. You must repay the original loan. In review, the tax savings from interest payments reinvested is worth about $24,000 (RRSP and open account). The tax owing on withdrawal for education will be about $16,000 if you remain in the 46% tax bracket.

In addition to tax-assisted saving, the beauty of this strategy is the low monthly cost of financing. If in the beginning, you had a small amount, say, $5,000 to open the account, and you borrowed $10,000, you'd have plenty in 18 years to cover all your child's education cost.

I've had friends who felt they had to mortgage their homes to send their children to university. That is a form of borrowing. Well, if you have to borrow, why not borrow now, write off all the interest cost and build your RRSPs at the same time?

Suggestion—or rather a warning

Leveraging is not for everybody. It is a strategy to use when you have excess cash flow, steady employment and a long-range investment horizon. It may also work particularly well when you have a spouse who is not working outside the home. You may wish to make spousal RRSP contributions and your spouse could later use some of that money to pay down the original loan. If you are in a situation like that, take heed of the three-year attribution rule on spousal RRSPs, which can involve extra tax.

Another form of leveraging for those who do not have $5,000 or $10,000 to start off with, is the match-your-RRSP program offered by some mutual fund firms. You may match, for example, a $250 per month RRSP contribution with a $250 per month interest-only investment loan. If you did this for 18 years your investment (if it returned 10%) would be worth $144,000. After repaying the loan of $54,000 you'd be left with about $90,000 which even after taxes would cover most of your child's education expenses. If the child does not opt for university, the money is yours—no strings attached. Such a strategy allows you to build a significant amount of money from fairly humble beginnings. At the peak of your borrowings, you would be paying about $360 per month, tax-deductible, if loan interest rates were 8%. (Note that RRSP-loan interest is not deductible.) You always have to have enough cash flow to weather higher interest rates, and you need a long-term investment horizon and a steady income. If your plans get this sophisticated, it's advisable to use the expertise of a professional financial planner.

As a professional planner I have come across some weird and wonderful schemes over the past 10 years. From leveraging borrowed money to leveraging equity in a home, clients and planners have tried to find the optimum way to financial success. My observations tell me that there is no single secret or magic in this regard, but there are basic premises most of us should live by:

- Start early.
- Invest for the long term.
- Save taxes when possible.
- Above all, don't get in over your head.
- Make sure you avoid the most common investment error of having the wrong investment objectives.

One of the better investments

Mutual funds are an excellent investment vehicle for education purposes.

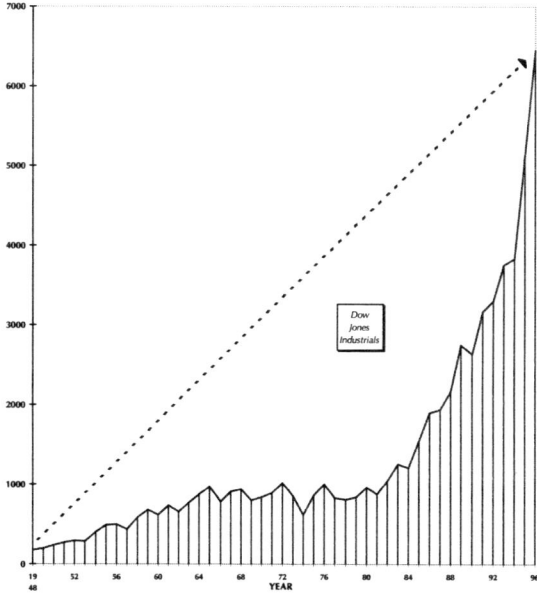

This is particularly true if you are making monthly contributions. If you invest the same amount each month in mutuals, that is called dollar-cost averaging. This is a great ally during fluctuating markets, and over the long term, it significantly reduces the risk of investing. If you are a conservative investor who simply must minimize risk, choose a conservative fund— it is extremely important to be comfortable with the way you invest. No amount of opportunity is worth not sleeping at night.

If you do choose a variable-rate investment such as mutual funds, know what you can expect over the long term. No fund will appreciate in value on a smooth, steady plane. Investment return will vary with stock-market movement and the economic environment, but the overall trend is upwards, as the Dow Jones graph above indicates (from *The Money Gap*). Don't become discouraged or fearful when your investment does not perform as you expected. Don't let your emotions dictate your investment strategy. Resolve and discipline are the keys to long-term investment success—that and a good financial planner who can help you sort through the financial clutter. Remember there is no easy way. I repeat: *make haste, slowly*.

A final admonition

Your best investment friend (and worst investment enemy) is time. Use time wisely; begin today, stick with your plan and time will provide the opportunity you need to build a substantial education fund for your children. Procrastinate for even one year and time begins to work against you. The less time to your goal, the more money you need to invest. The longer you wait, the greater the cost. Consider this : $2,000 per year invested for 18 years at 6% would amount to $65,520. If you wait until your child starts school and contribute for only 13 years, you'll need to invest $3,200 annually.

ED MACDERMAID is a former educator, a father of two university graduates and three other would-be graduates. He graduated from St. Thomas University in Fredericton, New Brunswick, and began a career teaching high school at Miramichi, N.B. (formerly Chatham). After 19 years he left teaching and in 1988 opened a Money Concepts Financial Planning Centre in Miramichi. It has become one of the most successful Money Concept franchises in Canada. Ed and 10 associates currently operate from the Bathurst, N.B., office that he opened in 1991.

During his career with Money Concepts, Ed has earned membership in the Chairman's Club every year since its inception in 1990. In addition to operating his planning business, Ed is the Money Concepts regional franchise developer for New Brunswick, president of the Money Concepts national organization (Franchisee Holdco), a member of Money Concepts Canada's board of directors as well as member of the board of National Financial Co.

When he is not working, Ed is an avid sports enthusiast. He has participated in national championships in baseball, hockey and curling. He is active in the community and has served on many committees, most recently as chairman of the Labatt 24 Hour Relay charity event.

Ed may be reached in Bathurst by telephone at 506-548-0808 and by fax at 506-548-2342.

12

Segregated Funds

They are finding their place in the sun
Because of a host of special features   By Noel Milner

egregated funds are really mutual funds—with a difference. Or rather, many differences. Those differences can make them more useful than regular mutual funds for investors with particular requirements.

Seg funds, as they are generally called, have been the prerogative of insurance companies, and until recently available only through them. They have been around for more than 30 years but only lately have started coming to the attention of average investors—so much so that mutual fund companies are including seg funds as part of their offerings. However, only licensed life insurance agents may sell them since they are life-insurance products. They are managed and invested like mutual funds, but the investments belong to the investor and are not part of the assets of the insurance company.

Seg funds are competing these days with mutual funds for the investment dollar and their market share is growing rapidly. That was not always the case. In the past, insurance companies weren't marketing their funds aggressively. At the same time, interest rates from guaranteed investments such as GICs were relatively high, and that offset one of the seg funds' main advantages. Also, seg fund investment managers tended to be conservative, salaried employees and had not developed a success-oriented reputation like many mutual fund managers had done. On top of this, most segregated funds didn't present the diversity of investments that mutual funds offered.

Things have changed. Now you may choose from a wide variety of segregated funds similar to the mutual-fund menu: money market, mortgage, bond, balanced, equity (both domestic and international), as well as index funds that follow the stock market indices. They are available on a front-end load basis where you pay commission at the time of purchase, or back-end load where commissions apply when you sell (based on a declining basis over five to seven years). Some insurance companies amortize these back-end fees from the initial investment date only, which is a distinct advantage over mutual funds that amortize fees based on each individual purchase date. Seg funds are also available on a no-load basis with no commissions payable either up front or upon redemption. No-load funds often, however, carry a higher, ongoing management fee that can make up for the lack of commissions.

Your investment is guaranteed, but you pay for that

One of seg funds' advantages for those needing it, is a guarantee, upon maturity, of 75% to 100% of the original investment regardless of how the investment has fared. Buyers pay for this warranty through a higher management fee charged by the insurance company—higher than most mutual-fund management fees. You pay a premium, so to speak, to insure your principal.

Maturity is commonly 10 years after you set up the program. The same guarantee of capital applies in the event an investor dies. Guarantees vary among companies and usually upon the age of the annuitant (the technical name of the seg-fund investor). The guarantee applies to the original principal less any payments or withdrawals since the inception of the plan. In the past year or so, some companies have introduced a reset provision that allows you to periodically reset the principal invested to include growth of your capital to that point, thus increasing the guaranteed amount.

Not everybody agrees

Critics of segregated funds say the extra fees are onerous, but many investors feel the guarantee provides a security that allows them to sleep comfortably at night. You can't put a price on that. The question of whether the "extra" management expense cost is adequate to fund the potential liability is being investigated as this book is written. Until industry actuaries substantiate that it is, some companies are holding their maturity guarantee to 75% and not moving to 100% as others have.

Cost is relative, of course. Many of our costs are lower today than in previous years and less expensive as a percentage of what we earn. You undoubtedly have run into people who fondly reminisce about times when you paid only 10¢ or 15¢ cents for a coffee and a donut. They often forget that in those days they only earned $2 a day, so as a percentage of income, you should be paying about $10 today for a coffee and a donut. Around $2 is today's going price.

If you were honest, you probably would admit that your main concern today should be how long your capital will last relative to how long you will live. If you have managed to squirrel away a retirement nest egg of $500,000, you might expect to get a pre-tax income of $27,500 annually at a 5.5% yield. That's not much. If you apply an inflation factor of just 1.25% per year, your capital will eventually become depleted, especially since we are now living much longer on average compared to previous generations. A greater growth potential is a major reason why some mutual funds initially, and now some segregated funds, are so rapidly growing in popularity. You can diversify your investments and expect to enjoy a 6% or 8% income draw while your invested capital still grows. A guaranteed initial investment provided by segregated funds is particularly important for many people. It allows them to buy more volatile, growth-oriented investments that may not only keep pace with inflation, but also surpass it.

Protection against creditors another seg-fund benefit

Since segregated funds are life insurance products, they are protected against creditors, as long as the courts do not decide that you entered into the contract for the express purpose of avoiding creditors. Often, the length of time you have owned the fund is important, though it is not the final determinant. The fact that creditors cannot get their hands on your assets is very important if you are an independent business owner and need to provide for your family and their future.

Bypassing probate is another benefit

Because you must name one beneficiary or more to fulfil the obligations of an insurance contract, the assets of a segregated fund will pass on directly to the beneficiary. This simplifies estate settlement and can save a lot of money in probate fees since the estate size may be significantly lower. If segregated funds are registered (as an RRSP), they can roll directly into your spouse's name. If the beneficiary is anyone else, the estate must pay tax before distributing assets to the named beneficiary.

Death-benefit guarantee a further advantage

While the protection of seg-fund guarantees does add cost, the opportunity to build your capital more aggressively, combined with protection, has led to their growing popularity during the past few years. The guarantees are not the same from all insurance companies. Some, for instance, offer 100% death-benefit guarantee but reduce it to 75% for money deposited after age 65. The guarantee builds up to 100% again after five years. It is important to check the fine print regarding the guarantee and you should expect the salesperson to describe it in detail and assess its suitability for your particular situation. There is no medical required for the guarantee, regardless of a client's medical history.

A prominent life insurance company recently determined through a study, that their clients valued potential creditor protection as the most important seg-fund advantage, followed by probate bypass, and lastly, the 100% death-benefit guarantee. The company concluded most clients felt that it would be hard to lose money during 10 years of investing, so the maturity guarantee was not as significant as it might seem.

Here is the cost structure

Management fees for segregated equity funds run from 0.5% to 3%. The guarantees add a further 0.5% to 1% to the cost. Taken together, these fees and expenses make up the fund's Management Expense Ratio, or MER. Despite the slightly higher cost, segregated funds with their guarantees, free withdrawal privileges, reset options and additional protection from The Canadian Life and Health Insurance Compensation Corporation (Comp Corp), are an attractive alternative investment opportunity. Comp Corp is a federally incorporated, private company consumer protection plan. Its objective is to protect, within limits, Canadian policyholders against loss of benefits should an insurance company member become insolvent. Both the maturity and death benefits are covered by this plan. Mutual funds are not covered by a consumer protection organization.

SEGREGATED VS. MUTUAL FUNDS: THE DIFFERENCE

	Segregated	Mutual
Structure	Insurance policy	Trust or corporation
How regulated	Insurance regulators	Securities regulators
Main disclosure doc.	Summary information folder	Prospectus
How sold	Insurance agents	Brokers/dealer, fund reps
Death-benefit guarantee	Up to 100%	None
Maturity guarantee	Up to 100% after 10 years	None
Creditor protection	Some. Depends on beneficiary	None
Probate fees	None	Probate fees payable

How seg funds helped a client with a special need

In 1994 a referral led me to a potential client. We'll call him Tom for simplicity's sake. The first two of three meetings were an examination of where he was at that time and where he wanted to be in the future, financially speaking.

He was just changing jobs. His former employer suggested he make arrangements to transfer his accumulated locked-in pension before he started his new job. *Locked-in* describes a pension under federal or provincial legislation. You cannot access its income until you reach age 55 or, in some cases, until the time the pension agreement allows for retirement. This restriction is an attempt by government to make income available as long as possible into retirement years and to avoid premature withdrawal and exhaustion of funds. One of Tom's main concerns was how to invest this pension money.

His locked-in pension was sizeable, but not enough to retire on. He was only 48 and though he knew little about his investment options, he knew retirement was not yet an option. He was married, his wife worked outside the home, they rented an apartment and their grown children lived elsewhere working at their own careers. Tom's pension represented the lion's share of their savings.

Tom's idea of retirement was freedom to do what he wanted, when he wanted. He was excited about starting his new business doing maintenance, repair and janitorial work. This would allow him to work as much or as little as he wanted; and he wanted to keep busy. He realized he would be especially busy at first dealing with the differences of being independent and working for himself. Since he was not used to dealing with money matters of this size, he was anxious to make a decision about the pension funds so he could move ahead with his new life.

Tom wanted his pension money to work for him right away. He also said he would like it to grow at a reasonable rate without risk of capital erosion. He was relying on my recommendations so I had to make sure I addressed all his concerns. We started with a financial needs analysis that examined his current situation and considered where he wanted to be when he retired. It also determined how much money he would need to live comfortably at that time.

Financial needs analysis told us a lot

He had $89,500 to work with and interest rates were currently on the decline. If things went well in his new career, he figured he wouldn't have to take income from his pension investments for about 10 years. We determined that if his money grew in a fixed-income, GIC-type investment, it would take the full 10 years to double. Would that be enough? A $180,000 asset 10 years later would provide him a pre-tax income of approximately $10,000 per year without touching the principal, assuming interest rates would stay at 6.5% or 7%. As it turned out, interest rates decreased, and there seemed little likelihood that they would go much higher in the near future. As with any registered investments (pensions, like RRSPs and RRIFs are considered registered), the growth (interest, dividend or capital gain) is tax-deferred. It is only later when you tap the income stream, regardless of type (annuity, RRIF, LIF), that it becomes taxable at your marginal tax rate.

We discussed three options before making a decision:

1. Transfer the pension to a locked-in, registered GIC. With a guaranteed principal and a return of 7%, it would take 10 years to double the investment.

2. Transfer the pension funds to a diversified, fairly conservative, mutual-fund portfolio that would not guarantee the principal but would eliminate ongoing investment decisions and at the same time provide greater growth opportunity.

3. Transfer the money to a segregated fund that would guarantee the principal and offer the opportunity for lucrative growth.

Tom wanted his money to work hard for him so he could retire before age 65. Because of the guarantee of principal, he felt the investment could be more aggressive, so he went with a single, segregated equity fund dealing in small- to mid-sized capitalized corporations. He felt he could diversify down the road, depending on the degree of growth the program attained.

The segregated-fund situation was ideal for Tom. The contract provided a guarantee of 100% of the principal invested, upon maturity (with this particular company it was 10 years–fairly standard in the industry). Also, the same guarantee applied upon the death of the fund owner, or annuitant to use segregated-fund terminology

The company offered withdrawal privileges

I checked with the life insurance company's segregated fund department before Tom signed. They were more than co-operative and agreed to issue an amendment for up to a 10% free withdrawal privilege per year in case Tom might need cash from time to time. This was a clause common to mutual funds but not to segregated funds at the time. The small-cap fund that the company had just bought was not large at that time (just a few million dollars) and it was investing in companies with capitalization of less than $300 million. We anticipated that such firms would be inclined to hire new employees as they grew rather than downsizing. They would be carrying less inventory than larger firms, and this type of organization was growing rapidly in the '90s.

The company Tom dealt with had other funds available, but I felt strongly that this new small-cap program would give my client a better growth opportunity, and still provide the security that he needed.

It was the right choice

Things went well from the beginning. I felt more and more confident as time went by. The investment was growing nicely. I met with my client regularly for reviews, and after two and a half years without a sign of the growth dropping off we decided it was time to diversify. The original $89,500 had grown to $172,800 by the November 1996 review.

I knew we were unlikely to continue this rate of growth forever and I was reluctant to stay entirely in the relatively volatile small-cap fund for too long. Tom's time frame was long term—10 years more or less, although he might need income in the medium term of five to nine years.

With this in mind I suggested he take $72,000 from the existing fund and split it among three other companies, but this time in more traditional mutual funds. We did this in December 1996. Now, about four years after we started the program, Tom has a diversified portfolio spread amongst more than 300 companies (through the funds) and it is already worth more than $225,000. If he had chosen the ultra-conservative GIC method of investing, he would be lucky to double his original investment by the year 2004.

Tom's pension is locked in for another two years (to age 55) but when he is allowed to withdraw income, he can look forward to more of it than he originally expected. He decided to keep his business going since he is enjoying it so much, and he will eventually use his pension account to enhance his retirement lifestyle. He could for instance, take longer and better holidays by making periodic withdrawals.

He'll have almost half-a-million by age 60

By the time Tom is age 60, and if his pension investments average 9% growth, he will have a $450,000 nest egg. That will be enough, if he wants to stop working, to generate an income of $2,300 per month *after tax*, without infringing on his capital. This amounts to an annual 8% income withdrawal.

The segregated-funds option allowed Tom to invest in growth markets while knowing his capital was safe. Rates of return from stock-market investment admittedly were abnormally high during this period, and small- to mid-cap corporations were especially favoured. But it was the underlying seg-fund guarantees that enabled Tom to develop a well-diversified portfolio that he was comfortable with.

The world, especially the investment world, is becoming the global village that communications guru Marshall McLuhan described. Accordingly, the rules have changed (which is not to say there won't be market corrections in the future) and investors are looking for new ways to make their money grow. Guaranteed investment certificates are no longer enough. Study after study tells us that baby boomers will continue to pour investment money into the economy until at least the year 2020. That money will stimulate the economy and investors will need to pick from an increasingly broader menu of choices. The market share of segregated funds will continue to grow. Perhaps they have a place today in your portfolio.

NOEL MILNER is president of the Money Concepts business in Cobourg, Ontario, which he opened in 1989. He graduated in 1971 from Ryerson Polytechnic University in Toronto with a business administration diploma, and worked for a financial institution in credit, operations and business development. In the mid-1970s he moved to commercial banking and a few years later started his own business in Cobourg, because "I wanted my family to grow up in a small town."

He sold that business and after a short stint as a much-travelled international sales manager, he began a successful career as a life, disability and group insurance broker with a major Canadian company. Noel found that his clientele grew and so did its needs. He recognized that Money Concepts could provide what his clients needed and in 1989 he became a self-employed, Money Concepts financial planner.

Noel has had a wide involvement in community affairs. He has chaired a professional theatre organization, been on the board and also president of the local YMCA and served as campaign chairman of the United Way. In 1994 he received the Bob Proctor Award for personal growth and development from Money Concepts.

He is married to Ene and they have two sons. Noel enjoys golfing in his spare time and trips on his motorcycle (he has a collection). He has a deep sense of commitment to family, business and community: "Always in that order." He is a practitioning member of the Canadian Association of Financial Planners.

Noel may be reached in Cobourg by telephone at 905-373-0300 and by fax at 905-373-0302.

13

Asset Allocation Is Far More Than Diversification

By Karl Murphy, BA & John Wilson, CFP

*P*roper portfolio diversification can reduce risk and bring a reasonably high return. Many clients and potential clients tell us, "I am diversified. My guaranteed investment certificates (GICs) are spread among five different banks."

Well, it is important to protect your GICs through the Canada Deposit Insurance (CDIC), but that's not diversification. You spread your GICs around because generally CDIC protection extends to your interest-bearing deposits at member financial institutions (usually banks, trust companies and credit unions) up to a maximum of only $60,000 per person per institution

Properly diversifying your investments goes well beyond spreading your investments among different companies. In fact, using different companies is not nearly as important as investing in different types of investments. In addition you must consider your risk tolerance and the factor of market timing. When a qualified financial planner helps you put all this together, you are participating in a modern—and fairly recent—investment approach known as asset allocation.

What are different investment types?

To start at the beginning we should examine what is meant by different types of investments. There are, generally speaking, three main types:

1. cash
2. fixed-income
3. Equity investments

CASH

Cash means more than cash. It includes anything you may easily redeem, such as money in savings accounts, Canada Savings Bonds and money-market mutual funds. Because savings categorized as cash are liquid, so easily redeemed and do not fluctuate in value, the interest rate they earn for you is quite low. (Check your bank account interest the next time you are there but prepare to be horrified.)

FIXED INCOME

Fixed-income investments offer the investor a consistent, periodic income stream. They could be bonds, mortgages or mutual funds that hold this type of investment. Even a balanced mutual fund, a conservative stock or dividend fund oriented more towards income than growth could be classified this way. You may expect a little better return from fixed-income investments than from cash; however you may also experience a little more fluctuation in the original capital value in the short term.

Unfortunately many investors in conservative mutual funds during the past few years were unaware that their capital amount could temporarily fall in value as well as rise. Searching for an investment with a better return than plummeting GICs, they were guided towards relatively low-risk mutuals. But low-risk does not mean no-risk. Values fluctuate though the volatility is low. The average investor makes little distinction among bonds, fixed-income funds and GICs. Until, that is, they see in the daily financial pages the fluctuating values of their bonds and mutual funds. If the value of their principal is down, investors start get nervous. The reality is that you don't lose money unless you redeem a fund. Shifting value is simply the price you must pay for the flexibility of being able to redeem a fund when interest rates go up. GICs, on the other hand, normally can't be cashed in before their maturity dates so their return appears absolutely fixed—until, that is, maturity time and they are faced with rolling them over to a lower-return GIC.

EQUITIES

Equities are evidence of ownership in something. The something could be a corporation, real estate, commodities or mutual funds that invest in any of these. The main goal of equity investment is growth of capital, although many equity investments also generate some regular income, usually through dividends. Many factors including a company's or other entity's profitability, financial stability as well as the investors' perceptions of these attributes affect the value of equities in a portfolio. Interest-rate increases or declines and the general economic climate also have a bearing on an equity's traded value. As a result, equity investments are subject to the greatest fluctuations in value of all investment types we mention here.

There are, of course, many sub-categories of both fixed-income and equity investments so far as mutual funds are concerned. Some of these are:

◆   **Special equity funds.** They consist of stocks of a particular industry sector or geographical area.

◆   **Real estate funds.** The values of these reflect the current health of the real estate industry at any given time.

◆   **Mortgage funds.** Their value usually fluctuates with interest rates. They are not risk-free.

◆   **Dividend funds.** Usually invested in blue-chip stocks with solid dividend histories. They can provide a steady income.

◆   **Index funds.** These trace exactly the investments of particular stock exchanges.

◆   **Asset allocation funds.** Developed by fund companies, they are a sophisticated version of the don't-put-all-your-eggs-in-one-basket school.

These options, while offering more choice, render diversification and asset allocation much more difficult and call for sophisticated advice. That brings us to an issue investors should concern themselves with. It arises in our office frequently. People come to us and want a quick answer as to what they should invest in and how much. Unless they are established clients, we always tell them that we can't answer that question until we know more about them. This holds true for any aspect of a personal financial plan, whether it be risk management and what and how much insurance to buy, or how much and how to save for your children's education.

If a financial advisor gives you a quick answer, be suspicious. It can mean he or she is bent on selling you something they happen to be promoting or have a direct interest in. You should prefer that your advisor supply you with what you need rather than what they want to sell–too often the special of the week. Be leery of quick answers to financial and investment questions, and especially about asset allocation. Now, before we actually get to allocating assets, we should touch on two factors that affect the process:

1. Risk.

2. The effect of time vs. market timing when buying and selling.

RISK

Many investors fear the word "risk." We do tend to fear what we don't understand, and this is usually the case when faced with managing risk. Additionally, risk means different things to different people. To some it's, "Am I going to lose all of my money?" To others it's, "Is there a chance I could lose any of my money?" These questions really boil down to, "How much will my investment go up and down in value?" In the investment world, ups and downs in the value of stocks are called volatility. Everyone perceives volatility differently. As investment professionals, we financial planners must consider a client's perception of what risk means to them, and their risk tolerance (which we can measure), when helping them build a portfolio designed for future financial peace of mind. Though we are looking at the long term, a client's current peace of mind is an important factor.

Many investors don't want to hear about risk at all. But they still want to get the high returns. Recently a potential client approached us (we'll call him Bob) and referred to a friend's investments. "I'm not sure what he invested in," Bob said, "but it's two mutual funds and he has doubled his money over the past three years. Would that be risky?" I told Bob that although I don't know what his friend's investments are, he would need an average return of 24%

$10,000 INITIAL INVESTMENT

Years	@10%	Years	@12%
7.2	$20,000	6	$20,000
14.4	40,000	12	$40,000
21.5	80,000	18	80,000
28.8	160,000	24	160,000
35	$320,000	36	$840,000

The yield your portfolio earns over the years is critical. This table shows the huge gap an extra 2% average return makes after 35–36 years of saving.

to double his capital in three years. That is obviously very good but you can't expect to maintain it for an extended period of time. The average returns on equity investments have been around 11% during the past 40 years or so. Of course, any one investment can beat the average. However, hitting a mere 2% over the average over time is significant. For example, the *Rule of 72* tells us that the number of times your rate of return will divide into 72 is approximately the number of years it will take your money to double. This table compares an investment of $10,000 at 10% to the same amount at 12%.

Double the final result for just another 2% return in about the same time! That's a lot.

Our point is that an average 24% return is highly unlikely over time. Some time in the future Bob's friend will likely experience significant corrections or backsliding (negative return) in his investments. That will probably bring his friend's earnings back to a more realistic, long-term figure. This may happen over time in small amounts or it could happen all at once like in the Asian markets during the fall of 1997.

So, if you are like Bob and big returns are attractive, you may want to examine ways to reduce your risk. Investments that look good now, such as those on top 10 lists that the financial pages love to publish regularly, can be misleading. As Grant Sylvester mentions in his best selling book, *The Money Gap*, "There is good evidence that to indicate that the majority of funds located in the top quartile of performance in any year are usually found in the bottom quartile the following year."

The moral of this story is stick to the long-term rules of asset allocation rather than grabbing what is hot today.

No such thing as a risk-free investment

Clients sometimes ask us to keep them in a risk-free investment environment. We can't. There is no such thing. There are varying degrees of risk from low through high, but none are risk free. "Hold on a minute," you might say. "What about GICs and savings accounts?" Well, these instruments appear to rule out the element of risk, but it depends how you define risk. A GIC or money in a savings account will not decrease in value and will give you a fixed return in interest. But will the $10,000 from a GIC buy the same thing in five or 10 years when you redeem it as it does today? Of course not. The cost of living goes up every year and income tax takes a bite out of the interest the

GIC pays each year. Inflation and taxes are subtle opponents an investor faces; they creep up on you, constantly chipping away at the value of your investments. The following is an example that occurs regularly:

Jane, who retires at age 55, has a 50% chance of living to age 84 according to current Statistics Canada. There is a 10% chance she'll need income past age 95. That means stretching her income out to 40 years. She has $200,000 invested and wants to draw an income of $8,000 per year from that. Jane would also like to leave the original $200,000 to her children. If she gets a 5% yield in interest she would have an income of $10,000 per year. No problem, then. Or is there?

Assume that inflation is 4%. Today's inflation rate is less than this, but the historical average is between 5% and 7%. Jane has the $200,000 in GICs returning 6% (a touch more than was being offered at this writing). At an income-tax rate of 30%, Jane will run out of money in the 26th year. That's not only not enough for her own life span but leaves nothing for her children. Risk is not always how you invest. As Sylvester says in *The Money Gap*, the biggest risk is often not taking any—and missing the opportunity of investment returns that would more than offset inflation and taxes.

To sum up, achieving your investment objectives is not simply going for the highest return available each and every year. If you are always trying to find a better return than everybody else, you will often be disappointed. If you are disappointed, you most likely will be switching advisors regularly. One of our biggest challenges is to help our clients understand what a realistic expectation of return actually is. An investor must understand how to balance risk against reality and consider the subtle players in the game: inflation and taxes. The rates of return that many investors chalked up during 1996 and 1997 won't likely reoccur, at least for some time. But memories of the big gains tend to stimulate both greed and high expectations. It's our job as prudent advisors to convince clients to forget the peaks and invest for the longer term consistent with their risk tolerance and circumstance.

TIME VS. TIMING

Some investors consider that success in investing like many other aspects of life lies in timing: being in the right place at the right time and buying the right stock or mutual fund at the right time and selling at the right time. Seldom considered, however, are the often-sad results of not being in the right place at the right time, and not having time to recover financially from a loss, before retirement. Though most people recognize the almost magical effect of compound interest steadily increasing an investment portfolio over time, not everybody tries to do it. A planner must acknowledge the roles of both time and timing in recommending a client's investment strategy.

Timing is extremely difficult. Its success is dependent on so many variables. For instance, it is almost impossible to predict when interest rates will rise or decline, quite apart from when the price of a particular stock will rise or fall off. But our experience has been that as average investors become more knowledgeable about their portfolios, the more questions they have and the more time-related these questions become. Seldom a day passes at our office that someone doesn't ask, "Where should I put my money?" And these days the questions are more often, "Where should I put my money now?" The answer to that question depends on what role time plays in your personalized financial plan.

Your financial plan is like a snowflake in that there are no two alike. Your plan reflects your uniqueness and the distinctiveness of your circumstances. For instance, your neighbour or relative does not necessarily expect to retire at the same age you do. And probably their anticipated retirement lifestyle doesn't resemble yours. Some retirees travel or move south for six months of the year; others are perfectly content to spend their time around home. Regardless of everybody's different visions, there are two constants that must be factored in when planning retirement: how much time do you have to prepare yourself for the type of retired life you want and how long do you expect retirement to last?" We must have answers to these questions before we can construct a proper allocation of your investment assets.

It's natural not to want to expose retirement savings to undue risk. At the same time, placing it all in GICs and running out of funds before you die is pretty risky too. Remember, retirement does not mean the end of your investment time horizon—it could continue for a very long time. So you must continue to include equity or growth type investments, of some proportion, in your portfolio.

How do you handle drops in the market?

When you have equities and even bonds in your portfolio, whether in the form of stocks or mutual funds, how do you avoid the invariable up-and-down roller coaster movements of the stock market? There will be short-term fluctuations, but keep your eye on the long-term average rate of return. While market fluctuations are natural, asset allocation models are attempts to choose investments that do not fluctuate in tandem—when one investment is down, the other is up. This is sometimes known as the risk-cancellation effect. By appropriately allocating your overall portfolio, you can endure the good and bad times in each area. The overall result is a smoother ride with above-average returns. Since it is virtually impossible to predict when the tides will turn and the markets will drop, you can take comfort in being prepared for any market fluctuations. You have taken some of the guesswork out of investing, which can cost you dearly.

Author and seminar leader George Hartman says, "Because investing is an inexact science, it is better to be approximately right, than precisely wrong." He was talking about effective asset allocation. As Grant Sylvester has pointed out in his book, studies show that more than 90% of the performance of a managed portfolio results from proper asset allocation, and less than 10% on the ability to choose high-performing individual assets. So tinkering with your investments to try for a few extra dollars in returns usually causes more harm than good. If you and your advisor have done your homework properly, asset allocation should leave you confident that your portfolio will do its job over time.

Implementing asset allocation

You must accept that there is a degree of risk in all investing, and that there is a difference between long- and short-term risk. We will recommend placing your assets among the three basic assets classes we discussed earlier with the goal of reducing risk and increasing return. To do the job properly we need the answers to a few questions since each investor is different and financial planners do not simply use just one mix or model of investments for all.

We need to know which of your goals and objectives are most important to you. For instance, do you want to retire at age 60? Do you want to pay for your children's education over the next 10 years? If you are retired now, do you want to get just enough to live on from your investments and leave a good chunk of money to your family as an inheritance? Or perhaps your prime focus is to build a nest egg to start a business five years from now.

We have to consider your time horizon. This includes your age and when you will start to need regular income from your investments (or the capital to start the business). Most people share a common belief that their time horizon is shorter than it truly is. A prime example is the person who says that they don't have long to invest because they will retire in a few years and will need the money. But few people will be retired for just one year. Most of us will face 30 to 40 years of retirement. These factors greatly influence how your portfolio will be allocated.

We have to get a measure of your risk tolerance, how comfortable you are with risk. Have you lost capital in the stock market in the past and has that made you gun shy? Will you be able to stick with your financial plan despite dips in the market? Once bitten, twice shy, and many investors don't have the stomach to see their capital shrink; they risk abandoning the plan.

Finally we assess your current financial situation because that plays a big role in deciding how much to allot to cash, fixed-income or equity investments. If your job situation is precarious, you may want to have more cash available for short-term emergency purposes. If you have a steady, fixed income from a pension or trust, you may not need as much in cash, or in fixed-income investments for that matter. You would weigh your portfolio more heavily toward growth assets or equity investments.

Determining the right mix of investments for your asset allocation is seldom a crystal clear process—asset allocation is not an exact science. Financial planners use general guidelines but for various reasons people don't always fit within these guidelines. So planners must use some personal judgement and experience to help make the investment mix fit the investor. That's part of a planner's job.

Here are three asset allocation models as examples

These sample asset-allocation portfolios will give you an idea of what is involved. Keep in mind that everybody's needs are different, and these general models would be further fine-tuned to each individual's particular circumstances. The three sample investment mixes are for aggressive, moderate and conservative investors.

MODEL ONE—AGGRESSIVE

This suggested portfolio mix would typically apply to a person just beginning a working life. It is evident that retirement is low on the list of immediate concerns. With 30 to 40 working years ahead to build a retirement fund and time to recover from stock-market setbacks, the recommendation is mainly for growth-type investments. The allocation assumes that emergency funds are already set aside and job security is intact, so safety of principal is usually not the highest priority. This is what an aggressive model might look like in percentages or pie-chart proportions:

AGGRESSIVE

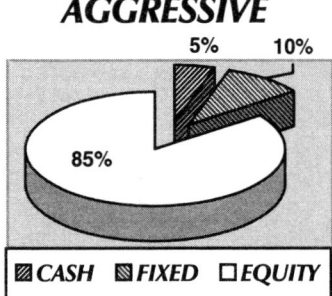

Cash:	5%
Fixed-income:	10%
Equities:	85%

• •

MODEL TWO—MODERATE

This recommended mix would typically apply to someone who is halfway through a working career. It features a more balanced approach of the three basic investment classes. Growth or equity holdings predominate, but you can see that the shift of assets has begun toward a larger fixed-income component, preparing for the onset of retirement.

MODERATE

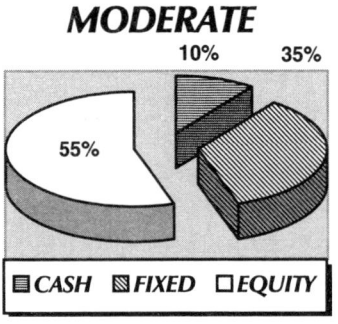

Cash	10%
Fixed	35%
Equities	55%

• •

MODEL 3—CONSERVATIVE

This mix would typically be for someone nearing or already enjoying retirement. Safety of principal plus a steady income stream are usually the key requirements for this type of client, so the portfolio holdings are weighted heavily towards fixed-income investments. Although small in size, there is still a growth-oriented component as well.

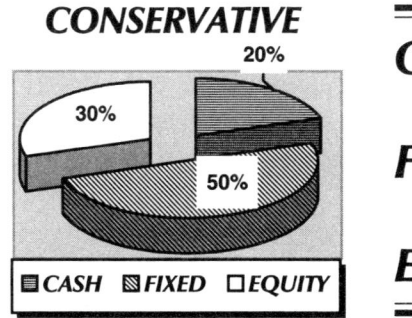

Cash	*20%*
Fixed	*50%*
Equities	*30%*

This has been an overview of asset allocation and we have just scratched the surface of the subject. A planning professional could go on at great length about foreign vs. domestic holdings, broad-based vs. specialty funds, and more. We cannot stress enough that these sample portfolios are benchmarks only. It is essential to use the expertise of your financial advisor to recommend further adjustments to suit your special circumstances. As we said earlier, everybody's needs and objectives are different, and your portfolio must reflect this. A financial planning professional who has an overview of the entire planning/risk management/investing process is the one to help you take the mystery out of asset allocation.

JOHN WILSON was educated in business administration at Sir Wilfrid Laurier University in Waterloo, Ontario, then joined the family service business in Renfrew and Pembroke where he looked after the administration and participated in company management.

In 1992 he joined Money Concepts and in 1994 he established

a company office in Renfrew. He soon earned his CFP designation and also holds an insurance license.

Away from the office, he is president of Renfrew Rotary Club and a member of United Church finance committee.

John and his wife, Margaret, have two young sons.

KARL MURPHY grew up in a family-owned-and-operated business and earned a BA from Carleton University in Ottawa. He later spent several years in a banking career before he moved to Money Concepts in 1995.

He enjoys skiing and is an experienced instructor. Karl is married and a member of the local Kinsmen club. He became partner of Renfrew Money Concepts office in 1997.

John and Karl may be reached by telephone at 613-432-5617 and 1-800-520-0820 and by fax at 613-432-2051.

14

What Your Pension Will (and Won't) Do for You

By Ed Thompson, B.Sc.A.

*T*oo few people pay much attention to their retirement's financial needs—until they are in their 40s. They suddenly find they have just 15 years to finish paying off the mortgage, put the children through college and set enough money aside for retirement. Forget about retiring at 55—they'll be lucky to retire at 65 with any amount of financial peace of mind.

Grant Sylvester said it in his book, *The Money Jar*: "Most people don't plan to fail, they just fail to plan." Too many people take politicians seriously and believe that the Canada Pension Plan (CPP) and Old Age Security (OAS) will carry them through. Others rely heavily on their employer's retirement pension plans. Few employees, though, examine the company plan closely to find out how good it is. It's often not until a few years before retirement that many employees discover how much income their pension will realistically provide at ages 55, 60 or 65. Even then, they don't always ask about pension portability, or what happens if they leave the company before retiring? Is their pension integrated with CPP and OAS and if so what will that mean happens to pension proceeds? Do they know whether their spouse will continue to receive income should they die first?

When I was age 24, I believed that my company pension plan would be my retirement ticket. I didn't bother to ask for and read the details about the coverage. Was that a mistake! If you want a financially comfortable retirement you must understand how your pension works. You must acquire this understanding well before you will need it, so you may take whatever action is appropriate. You must take responsibility and be in charge of your own retirement arrangements.

Two main types of pensions

There are two types of pension plans that companies provide to their employees: *defined benefit* and *defined contribution*. Defined benefit specifies in advance the benefit an employee will receive at a certain age or years of service. The employer (if it doesn't become bankrupt) is obligated to have the funding in place to pay the benefit and is responsible to do so— regardless of how the investments in the pension fund have performed. In a defined-contribution plan, the contribution amount is defined but the employer does not have the responsibility or the obligation to pay an employee a pre-specified benefit at retirement. Usually both employer and employee contribute to this type of plan, but the employee, not the employer, takes the risk on the amount of the final payout based on how the plan's investments work out.

Group RRSPs, which may be used as an informal type of pension plan in a company, are similar to defined-contribution plans, but do not fall under pension legislation.

There is a definite movement in the corporate world away from defined benefit plans to defined-contribution plans or groups RRSPs, so you should be aware how your pension plans works and what it will (and won't) do for you.

DEFINED BENEFIT PLANS

Knowing in advance how much income you'll get in retirement can give you a nice, secure feeling. But have you bothered to find out exactly how much that will be and what outside factors may affect it? As I mentioned before, too many people leave it until it is too late to take much remedial action. I know from first-hand experience. I started a career in 1967 with a large Canadian resource-type company that had a great benefit package; it included a company-funded defined-benefit pension plan. At the age of 23 I figured my retirement was already in the bag. Was I ever wrong! At age 28 I received a good offer from a large integrated oil company and took the new job. Guess how much my first employer paid me from the pension plan? Almost $550: a bonanza. This apparently was my plan's accumulation after five years. Since I hadn't figured on retiring at age 28, it never occurred to me to calculate in advance out how little I would get if I left before retirement. The great thing (at the time) was that they paid the bonanza to me in cash. So I was able to spend it. RRSPs I hadn't heard of yet.

My new employer was also a large company with an attractive employee benefit package. This also included a company-funded pension plan. Again my retirement was looked after so I didn't have to worry about putting money aside—Mother Company was looking after me. I would get a retirement income based on the average salary from my last seven working years, times years of service, times 2%. Since I was 28, I reckoned that in 30 years when I would be 58, I'd get 60% of my last few years average salary. And I'd get that for the rest of my life. I wouldn't have to put in a cent myself. This was great. It wasn't until I became a financial planner that I discovered the company's plan back then was a defined-benefit pension. The eventual payment was defined and predetermined and the company had an obligation to pay it when the time came. All I had to do was stay with that same firm for 30 to 35 years and I would retire on easy street. Since I really enjoyed the work I was doing, this appeared to be a sure thing.

Things change

After 16 years I wasn't enjoying the work so much. In 1988, drawing an annual salary of $65,000, I left to start a new career in personal financial planning. It didn't occur to me to ask the company how much pension I'd take with me; I just assumed it would be a fair amount. Then I learned that the pension adjustment (PA) spelled out on my T4 slip was about $5,500 per year. That seriously restricted me from adding much to my RRSP. No problem, I thought, my previous company must be putting $5,500 per year into my pension on my behalf.

How wrong can you be? I soon found that my pension after 16 years of service would eventually be slightly more than $22,000—about a third of one year's salary. After working 21 years I suddenly learned how defined-benefit plans work. And what about that $5,500 PA? Well, it never was, in reality. This was simply a figure formulated by the pension commission based on the assumption that you would stay with the same company forever. Pension adjustments at that time had no hard cash behind them—some actuary made the determination and I had thought nothing more about it. In essence, people who left their employer for another job after just a few years were treated as castoffs as far as PAs went. These days you may have the pension adjustment shortfall added to your RRSP contribution room if you change employers. Recent legislation acknowledges that the pension adjustment for defined benefit as stated on the employee's T4 slip, was not the actual contribution to the plan. For employees younger than age 40, it was substantially less. The legislation now allows what is called a Pension Adjustment Reversal (PAR). It must come in the form of a T10 slip from a pension plan administrator who forwards it to Revenue Canada which then may increase the RRSP contribution allotment. Unfortunately, some plan administrators do not seem to be aware of this change. To make sure it is done, you should pursue PAR with your former employer's plan administrators. Deferred profit sharing plans (DPSPs) also may trigger PARs.

Ironically, my former company also had an excellent share-purchase program in which they matched each dollar I put in, up to 5% of salary. When I left, that amounted to $30,000. I had done this mainly for fun and to satisfy my interest in investing. My pension was the serious item though, and I considered it to be my main asset. What a shock I got.

If you stay forever, it's the best

There is little doubt that defined-benefit plans are superior if the employee stays with the same company to retirement. An employee is at risk only if the company falls into financial difficulty and/or has to lay off staff to survive. Many employers, however, are not anxious that employees hang around for 30 to 35 years—it adds to the firm's pension costs especially during the last few years of an employee's work life. Conversely, how many employees these days want to stay with a single employer their entire career?

Why was my pension amount so small when I left?

A company setting up a defined-benefit plan must have an actuary on staff. The actuary's job is to calculate the company's obligations for funding the financial requirements of the plan. The actuary takes into consideration the number of employees, their ages, years of service and income. The object is to advise management how many dollars it must have in the plan to meet the defined-benefit obligation to employees as they retire. The actuary also looks at projected salary increases, employee turnover, employee death rates, inflation, annuity returns and projected workforce numbers. Management must know how much money it will need to fund an annuity to meet each employee's monthly pension.

Once the actuary is done, the company may find the pension plan is under-funded and it must inject more money. Or it might have an over-funded pension. If there is an over-funded plan, the company usually feels it owns the excess and may take it out if it wants—the T. Eaton Co. did just that a few years ago. In fairness, the employer takes all the investment risk and must make up any plan shortfall if one occurs. So it justifiably feels it should reap the rewards if it takes the risks.

It is in the company's interest to ensure the pension investments do well. A plan that grows 10% annually will require much less funding from the company than a plan returning 5%. The other part of the equation is the annuity return. Around 1990 and 1991 I recall selling life annuities yielding 12%. Each $10,000 annuity guaranteed a $1,200 annual payout until death. At today's interest levels it would probably take around $17,000 to fund that same $1,200 monthly payout. It's obviously in a corporation's best interest to have effective investment-management companies run their pension-plan portfolio: the higher investment returns, the lower the company's annual contribution would have to be.

The case for under-funding

A lot of pension plans are under-funded, and for a reason. Most actuaries will advise their companies that the plan does not require much funding for under age-45 employees who may die or leave the company before retirement age. Once they are over 45, however, there is a good chance they will stay until retirement, so the company's obligation to the pension plan starts to increase substantially for that individual. When a lot of employees reach that age level, a defined-benefit plan often becomes under-funded.

In some cases companies, rather than putting more money into the plan, opt for downsizing. I see this happen to a lot of clients who reach their mid-40s. Their performance doesn't seem to matter as much to the company any more. Often they become unhappy at work and quit or take early retirement. Some are hired back on contract so there is no pension obligation. In some ways, severance packages can be reasonable and allow a former employee to start a new career in another field of interest. The employer usually can replace the 40-plus employee with somebody younger—and at a lower salary. This way it won't have to pay the former employee a high salary for another 10 years and at the same time won't have to top up increasingly higher defined-benefit obligations.

Defined-benefit plans may also discourage companies from hiring older employees because of the soaring funding obligations of the plan during the last few years of an employee's corporate life. Changing a workforce to younger and fewer employees is one of the most effective ways for a company to eliminate a shortfall pension-funding obligation.

They cater to the average

A further problem, from the employee point of view, is that defined-benefit plans operate for the group as a whole, not the individual member. For example, the majority of the plan's members may be close to retirement so the trustees adopt a conservative investment approach designed to generate income for retirement. This could prove unfair to the younger employee-member who has a long way to retirement and perhaps needs a more aggressive investment strategy resulting in a lot of capital growth. From an administrative standpoint, and perhaps a trustee one as well, it's difficult to separate contributions and track investments by age groups by using several different investment guidelines. Sometimes this may be addressed by having more than one investment manager, especially if the pension fund is large enough to support that luxury. If a fund starts to exceed $350 million, often a second manager is brought on board. It's hard to satisfy everybody with pension management, and often the aim is to serve the whole group as a single entity: not necessarily satisfactory for every employee.

I don't blame companies for adopting defined-benefit pensions. Long-term employees do very well. Ones who leave early do not. These days the trend seems to be changing career paths five to seven times during a working lifetime. Defined-benefit plans obviously aren't the best fit in that case. Companies are starting to change their outlook on pensions since they aren't likely to be able to keep staff for 30-year careers. More employers are considering a switch to defined-contribution plans or RRSP group plans. These plans demand that the employee become more involved with their pension plans, and contribute advice to—even make decisions about—the plan's investments.

DEFINED-CONTRIBUTION PLANS

Pension plans of the future are likely to be transferable, defined-contribution plans or even group RRSPs. The employer is obliged to contribute to a defined-contribution plan but is not responsible for the investment outcome or payouts. This approach does have its drawbacks; for instance, the investment choices available to the employee are somewhat restrictive. Frequently the employer decides which financial company will supply the investments the employees may buy for the plan. Usually the employer (often in conjunction with the supplying firm) decides on the commonly circumscribed range of investments available to the employee. There are advantages to the employee: if your investments do well, you reap all the benefit. At any time, an employee may calculate how much the pension will amount to by taking the plan's current value to a financial planner. The planner can make the appropriate projections and give the employee an idea as to whether they will achieve their ultimate financial objective.

When you leave one employer for another, you have two choices regarding your defined-contribution plan: you may transfer your plan contents to a locked-in retirement account (LIRA) or you may be able to transfer them to the new employer's defined-contribution plan. The former means your pension funds are locked in until a specified retirement age. The latter means you would likely have to convert your previous plan into cash, then buy into the new employer's plan. In one way, contribution plans are less rigid. But they place the responsibility for investment success on the shoulders of the employee.

GROUP RRSPs

RRSP group plans do not fall under pension legislation, but they are often used rather than a formal pension plan. They usually are contributory plans but the contributions are not defined unless the employer makes it a condition. Group RRSPs are flexible and have advantages for both employer and employee. Neither party is under any obligation to contribute on a regular basis. You put money in on a when-available basis. It might be considered a disadvantage that employees may take money out to use as a sort of emergency fund. Unless the government institutes rules to restrict withdrawals, and to make group RRSPs creditor proof, there is a risk that the proceeds of a group RRSP at retirement will be inadequate for most people.

How much will you need?

How much money will you need at retirement? That's a question I am asked almost every day. One rule of thumb to determine adequate income at retirement is to take the annual amount you need today, in today's dollars, adjust it for inflation at age 60, then multiply that number by 22. For example, $30,000 of income for someone age 30 at a 3% inflation rate would be $72,818. Multiply this by 22 and that comes to $1,601,932. This is the amount you'd have to save by retirement to generate the income you want. That translates to putting away $8,853 each year in an RRSP that returns 10% on average. If your RRSP earned only 5% over the same period, you'd need to sock away $22,963 each year. If you could get a growth of 12%, you'd need to save only $5,927 annually.

Pensions alone will not likely produce enough retirement income for comfortable living. You probably will have to augment pension income with earnings from a personal RRSP. To help put it all together, you should use the expertise of a qualified, professional financial planner. Among other things, a planner will help you to learn how to accept the level of risk required to attain your objectives with the dollars you have available. The operative word here is help; ultimately the discipline and responsibility is all yours to make happen. You might have to make some hard choices when you set priorities during the personal financial-planning process, but with solid planning and strategic product selection, financial independence can become a retirement reality.

EDWARD L. THOMPSON is president of a Money Concepts business in Winnipeg, which he opened in 1988. He was born and raised in rural Manitoba and in 1967 attained a Bachelor of Science degree in agriculture from the University of Manitoba. He has since completed the work required for his chartered financial planner (CFP) designation and is a member of the Canadian Association of Financial Planners. He is a member of the Money Concepts National Financial advisory council.

Before he became a professional financial planner, Ed worked in marketing for two major agricultural suppliers. He has carried forward to his planning career his keen interest in marketing and investing that he developed earlier. Though he applies his money-management expertise to a broad range of clients, Ed tends to focus on those in business and agriculture because of his extensive background in those fields. His business style is to develop personal and lasting relationships with clients.

He is a member of several professional agricultural organizations such as the Manitoba Institute of Agrologists and the Canadian Agricultural Marketing Association. He is actively immersed in the community as past-president and now treasurer of the Charleswood Rotary Club. He has also coached children's activities at his local community club and has participated in fund-raising there.

Ed is married to Elaine and they have two children. Outside the office, he enjoys golfing, sailing and camping in the family motorhome.

Ed may be reached in Winnipeg by telephone at 204-832-9148 and by fax at 204-896-5907. His e-mail address is: ed@money.mgmt.com.

15

Disability Insurance: The Most Important of All?

By Peter Tiani, CFP, RFP

*I*f you met me, you would immediately know why disability insurance should be an essential part of everybody's personal financial plan. The first thing you'd notice is that I have only one arm. My other arm is artificial and ends in a metal hook—I lost it in an accident when I was 21 years old. That's when I became aware of the value of disability insurance—and the shortcomings of many companies' group benefit plans.

My personal experience has shown me how vital disability insurance (often known as income-replacement insurance) is for most people—individuals or small business owners. Yet hardly anybody I talk to about their financial future has given any thought to the possibility of becoming disabled. Those who have, tend to slough it off as too expensive.

It may not be cheap. And it is complicated, perhaps the most complicated of all insurances. That's another reason, perhaps, that many planners do not deal with it thoroughly—because they do not have the expertise.

But is that enough reason to ignore it? Consider these figures: The Society of Actuaries, in its 1985 DTS table, points out that of 1,000 people, the number disabled for three months or more before age 65, is:

At Age:	
25	6 out of 10 people
30	6 out of 10
35	1 out of 2
40	1 out of 2
45	1 out of 2
50	1 out of 3

Almost half of those who are still disabled after six months will continue to be disabled at least to the end of five years; this applies to most all ages.

As Grant and Rob Sylvester wrote in their book, *The Money Gap*, "... since we are living longer on average, than our parents and certainly our grandparents, thanks to better nutrition, sanitation and medical advances," nobody today can ignore the possibility they will suddenly become disabled. In fact, the Sylvesters say, between 1960 and 1979, 73% fewer men and women died from hypertension (blood pressure problems) and 70% more became disabled. One in 12 Canadians, they point out, is technically disabled at any given time these days. You cannot afford to dismiss disability insurance as part of your financial plan.

Planning is more than insurance

Of course, there is much more to a financial plan than disability insurance. A good plan consists of the six-step process (after you acquire a good planner):

1.   A snapshot of where are you right now and assembling the data to show you (cash management, net worth (assets minus liabilities), cash flow projections etc.).

2.   Picking your retirement age and discussing your goals and objectives (often the toughest part of planning).

3.   Evaluating your needs (life insurance, children's education, capital accumulation planning, investment analysis, etc.).

4.   Putting a plan and recommendations on paper.

5.   Implementing the plan.

6.   Conducting annual (at least) reviews.

I like to tell my clients about the three financial evils that could befall them:

1—Live too long and run out of money before you become an angel. It's very difficult to find a new job at age 75.

2—Die too soon. What happens to your partner or spouse, financially?

3—Become disabled sometime before retirement . This is worst of all because not only has your income stopped, the expenses keep coming in. In fact, the expenses could increase because you might have to modify your home to accommodate the disability (ramps, elevators etc.). People usually think that retirement planning stops at wealth accumulation and life-insurance coverage (though often they make no analysis of how much they require). The client and too often the planner overlook disability.

My experience has taught me not to make that oversight. My accident at 21 was in a car. I lost my right arm and suffered severe spinal-cord damage. Rehabilitation time was long and expensive. I had been a labourer in sawmill for a good company that treated me well and with respect. The only insurance coverage I had was through the company's group-benefit package. I had never thought of the possibility of disability, and very little about what the overall benefits were. I had never read the employee benefit booklet; in fact I didn't even know where it was.

At 21 you think you are bulletproof. Why would you read stuff about pensions and accidents at that age? You have the vague knowledge that you are covered in a big company's plan and the details aren't important. But I found later the details are important, very important.

Benefits cut off

I was in rehab at Vancouver for nine months (it should have been a year) in two of the best centres in the province, learning how to walk again and how to write again. During that period I felt it was a good time to make a career change. I enjoyed my work but I realized it would have been difficult to continue at the same job because of my injuries, even though my employer was willing to change things around so I could function with one arm. I started a two-year retraining program, the first year overlapping with rehab. Near the start of the second year I lost my benefits from the company plan, not because the employer was a mean one, but simply because of the way the contract was written.

Had I been aware of the group-benefit coverage limitations I might have augmented the company plan with outside, individual coverage. Fortunately I was able to live with my parents while I went back to school. I was single with no children. If this had happened to me later in life when I was married and a parent, that option of returning home probably would not have existed. So I was lucky and I want to pass along what I learned to as many people as possible: you must protect your income stream. You could lose it any time, without warning.

Disability can be even more devastating if you are in business for yourself or perhaps in a partnership. We will look at the business side of disability a little later in these pages.

As soon as I begin discussing disability insurance with clients, they all say the same thing: "But it's so expensive." Yes it is. But I point out to them that they don't hesitate to spend $1,400 a year (in British Columbia) to insure a car that is worth $30,000 or less. Most are spending $3,000 to insure two cars. They insure with little reluctance, sometimes at considerable cost, what they consider to be their largest asset, be it a boat or a home. Most of them don't realize until I point it out, that their biggest asset is the ability to get out of bed each morning and go out and earn an income for a few more decades.

Then I ask them to imagine that they have a printing press in their basements, which month after month and year after year turns out $50,000 or $70,000 a year (drop your own income figure in here) for them. It even prints a little more money each year to match inflation. Would they be willing to insure this money machine? The answer is invariably, Yes. That's insuring your income stream.

Remember disability insurance is not like winning the lottery. You don't get a big windfall when you become disabled; you get replacement income. And don't confuse disability insurance with accident insurance—93% of people become disabled because of sickness, not accident. That's why accident insurance is so cheap.

Disability (accident and sickness) insurance may not be cheap. It can cost more than life insurance. But look at the potential payout compared to life insurance if you have the right type of policy in place. It allows you to carry on with your usual lifestyle and also with your retirement and estate plans. Potentially a disability policy could pay you until you reach age 65, even if you retire at 55.

The cost is low relative to the benefits

The cost may be high but not compared to the potential payout. And you can tailor a disability policy to fit your income and circumstance. When you can afford more, you could augment the coverage.

One reason people don't opt for disability coverage is that it is complicated; there is much more fine print to read and many more choices to make than with most life insurance. You need to consult with an expert more than you do with life or general (car) insurance because of its permutations and combinations. Also, because they could pay out a great deal over the years, insuring companies check closely who you are and how much you have been earning as indicated on your tax returns when you apply for a policy. They make a detailed investigation to come up with the amount of coverage they allow you to buy.

Various sources of disability income

There are five sources of disability income for sick or injured Canadians who can't work, and for those who can still work but whose income has been reduced because of disability:

1. Canada/Quebec Pension Plan (CPP/QPP) disability benefits
2. Employment Insurance (EI) disability benefits
3. Worker's compensation benefits
4. Group disability insurance (from employers)
5. Individual disability policy including association coverage

1. CPP/QPP benefits are extremely difficult to qualify for. There are tight definitions of severe and prolonged disability. Severe means you can't work regularly at anything that pays. Prolonged means you are likely to be disabled indefinitely, or the disablement is likely to result in death. Here is what the 1999 benefits are:

♦ $903.55 per month plus $171.33 per child (outside Quebec)
♦ $903.55 per month plus $53.91 per child (in Quebec)

2. Employment Insurance benefits continue for 15 weeks after a two-week waiting period. Not a lot.

3. Worker's compensation benefits must stem from an injury or sickness suffered at work or a work-related activity. An accident at work is relatively easy to prove. Sickness is a vaguer concept. I had a client who worked in a local sawmill doing a repetitive job. After 16 years his shoulder wore out. He had to fight to prove that it was a work-related incident. In the end, since he was 55, he was allowed only 50% benefits because they ruled that half the injury was caused by age.

4. Group benefits, the type offered by companies to employees.

This is what I had at age 21. Employees often are aware there is disability coverage in their package, but they don't know the details such as what is covered, how much it is and how long it lasts. Unless you know and understand what you qualify for, you can be burned just as I was. I suggest to most people to thoroughly read their group-benefit package–not just the dental and medical coverage. The most important part is the disability coverage.

Most company disability plans have both short- and long-term coverage. The short-term component covers the first 24 months of your *regular* occupation. After 24 months, the definition of disability often changes: from your regular occupation to *any* occupation. This is a significant change and usually limits what you receive. The *any*-occupation condition means if you are employable to do anything, benefits would stop. If you can accept that, fine. Most employees don't realize they could be subject to this modification.

5. Individual disability contracts. These you buy individually through an agent or insurance company. In my case I could have had better coverage. Let's look at some of the many choices offered, the fine print and many of the options that are available with individual disability policies.

Typically, there are three types:

1. Commercial policies (accident only). These are often offered through mail order as a perceived benefit for buying a company's product or service, like fur steering-wheel covers offered by an oil company on its monthly statement. The insurance company may cancel coverage at any time, or increase premiums and add limitations. They are usually low in cost but you get what you pay for. If you can afford better coverage, do so. It is better than nothing, but not much.

2. Guaranteed renewable policy. This is a giant step forward from number 1. The insurance company guarantees it will renew your policy, typically until about age 55 though some will go longer. The drawback is that the company may still increase the premium at any time. It's light years ahead because it can be renewed and the insurer can't add riders and change wording to limit coverage later on.

3. Non-cancellable and renewable policies. This is the best. Rock solid. The insurer can't make any changes that would affect the holder detrimentally. It can change the policy to include new and better coverage and could reduce premiums, but it can't introduce anything that would affect the policyholder negatively even if that person switches to a more hazardous occupation. This is top-of-the-line coverage.

You need two things to buy these policies: health and some wealth. Let's look at the *guaranteed renewable non-cancellable contract* in more detail:

♦ The occupational classification you are in helps determine the premium. There are usually four or five different categories including smoker/ non-smoker, male/female. The more hazardous the job, in the insurer's eyes, the higher the premium.

♦ Benefit period means the length of time the payments continue once you are on claim. Every policy can be tailored to need, but they are typically 24 or 60 months, or 10 years or to age 65. The longer the period, the more expensive the premium.

♦ Elimination period is the time you wait before the benefits kick in. This could be after 14 days, 30, 60, 120 days or more. The sooner the benefits start, the more costly the premiums.

♦ Definitions of disability. Three words can change the meaning and the pricing of the policy:

1. Own. You are covered for your *own* occupation. You must be able to perform exactly the same work you did before or you receive full benefits.

2. Regular. This means *regular* occupation. Translated it means that if you are able to perform the main duties of your previous occupation, you don't get benefits. It's a wider definition and reduces the premium cost.

3. Any. This is a looser definition and less costly coverage. If you are able to pursue *any* occupation for which you are suited by training, education or experience after becoming disabled, you will not get benefits.

♦ Residual benefits. Some policies ignore occupation entirely and will pay full benefit if you lose 75% to 80% of your pre-disability income. This makes sense. Say you are off for six or seven months, and when return to work you have lost some accounts or clients. Thus your income had dropped by, for example, 40%. The residual benefit clause would make up that 40%.

♦ Partial disability. You may be able to go back to work for three hours a day rather than the usual eight. You get compensation for the three hours, but not the other five. If your contract reads that you must be totally disabled before you collect, you won't receive anything. This is an important factor, and it adds to the premium cost.

♦ Inflation indexing. If you are off for 10 or 20 years and your benefit starts, for example, at $4,000 a month, you will be okay for the early years, but not when the cost of living goes up as time passes. You need an inflation-index rider to stop your purchasing power from eroding each year. This is especially useful on a policy that pays for more than five years.

♦   Waiver of premium. Companies offering this rider waive the cost of further premiums after 90 days of disability.

♦   Recurrent disabilities. Usually any reoccurrence of a disability within six months of completing a claim is considered a continuation, so there would be no elimination or waiting period to go through.

♦   Lifetime benefit. This is particularly useful if you had not done any other retirement planning, or saved much towards retirement, and you need the benefits to continue beyond age 65.

♦   Future insurability. This means you could add to your coverage later if you have the income to support it. This increases your premium, but you wouldn't have to submit medical evidence later (though you do have to submit financial evidence to back up your income level).

♦   Own occupation rider. This is especially important for a professional such as a doctor or lawyer, or even a financial planner. You'd get full benefits if you couldn't return to the exact same job you were doing before your injury or illness. A surgeon would be a good example. There is likely no such thing as a one-handed surgeon. Without this rider the insurer would assume the surgeon could work within the medical field as a teacher or researcher, etc., and earn income.

What would I buy?

There are a lot of variations in disability contracts and you really need an expert to guide you through them. There is far too much detail to examine further in this chapter. Each person is different. Make sure you deal with an expert, not a generalist.

If I were buying a disability contract today, I would want to make sure that I had at least a guaranteed, renewable, non-cancellable coverage that starts after a reasonably short waiting time and would pay me for a good, long time. I would want coverage for my *own* occupation.

Comprehensive coverage: Expensive? Perhaps. But compare it to the cost of insuring other things: your home, car, cottage, boat etc. A lot less, relatively speaking. If you lose your income, you put in jeopardy that car, and your home, your cottage and your boat because you probably won't be able to keep the payments up, to say nothing of the premiums to insure them. Disability is the father and mother of insurances. It must be an essential component of your financial plan.

Disability and overhead insurance for the business owner

It is even more important for a business owner to have disability insurance than for an individual. A shareholder's agreement should not just cover death of a partner—disability is just as, or more, important. Businesses almost always have continuing liabilities to meet and sometime disability insurance is the only way to do it. Here are a few options to look at and a few common problems:

You could close a business if you become disabled, but usually there are bills to pay if you do that—rent, utilities, salaries to others for a while.

Or you might want to keep it open long enough and healthy enough so you don't have to sell it at fire-sale prices just before a deadline. It costs money to keep it going.

Disability-income insurance for a business will pay the business expenses even if the owner is gone. It covers such overhead items as telephone, rent and salaries for employees while you are in your recovery period. Often a business is an individual's largest asset and one they planned to capitalize on in later years by selling it to provide retirement income. The disability of the owner, key employee or key shareholder could be a catastrophe and the business might not survive.

Partners need it, too

Disability insurance is essential if you are sole proprietor or a key shareholder, but also in a partnership. If one partner becomes disabled, it could be a real problem. The partner could be away for a month or two and not be missed much, but if the disability is prolonged or long term, you need insurance. This needs to be addressed in a shareholder agreement and, as pointed out earlier in this book, preferably agreed to before the business starts. When you are disabled and perhaps not in a solid emotional state, it's no time to make decisions.

A disabled partner might come back, after several years away, to a business that is worth a lot more—growth they had no hand in developing. In fairness to those who continued, often the solution is to buy the disabled partner out, usually after it is determined that the stay away will be a long one. The question is then how to fund that buyout. If you can't fund it with your own cash or from the cash flow of the business (in which case you might restrict the business growth), disability buyout is the answer. The shareholder agreement must spell out the date when this is invoked: after a year or 18 months. Perhaps after 24 months.

A disabled person might well wish to be bought out, because he or she would not be on hand to help make the decisions that would assure the business remains healthy. You would have to rely on a partner or other shareholder. That's fine if their decisions are effective, but you might not agree with what they are doing. If they should run the business into the ground, you would still be responsible for its debts, even if you are disabled. So it's important from both sides of a partnership: the healthy and the unhealthy.

To give you an idea of how it works, my partner and I decided to have coverage for 18 months. As soon as one of us is off for 30 days, the business-overhead part of the contract kicks in, in our case for the following 17 months. At 18 months, if the person is still disabled, the buyout clause kicks in at a predetermined price. That is drafted into our shareholder agreement.

If this happens and I am the disabled one, I will have the proceeds of the buyout for investment purposes, along with the proceeds of my own personal disability policy to keep me going. Perhaps I will recover later on and my partner might hire me back or let me buy back in. If not, I could start a different business. It's a fair, equitable and affordable way for partners to act. Neither of us could afford to do this without disability insurance.

Peace of mind is the goal

In the end, the entire point of the financial planning process is to provide peace of mind. Without disability insurance—whether an individual or a business owner—you can't have complete financial peace of mind. It's difficult to know what your group benefits at work will provide. Often it will not be enough and you need expert advice to help you top up. A qualified planner can interpret your group benefits for you so you can make informed decisions. Remember, when you leave that group, typically the benefits will stop so you are back at square one as far as disability benefits are concerned. If you have an augmented personal plan in place, you'll have something when you leave.

You still might endure pain and suffering when you are disabled, but it will be a lot less stressful lying in that hospital bed knowing you are covered for personal and/or business disability insurance. You'll be confident that the incomes for your family and your business are still healthy even though you are not.

PETER TIANI is a partner in the Money Concepts Prince George, B.C., office. He worked for many years in the forestry industry then moved into accounting. He was involved extensively with personal and corporate tax, financial statement preparation and analysis and auditing. He has a diploma in accounting and finance, and the professional designations of Certified Financial Planner and Registered Financial Planner. He also has mutual fund, life insurance and accident and sickness licenses.

He undertakes the usual comprehensive financial planning functions, such as estate planning and protection, business planning and succession, retirement and investment, education and tax planning. Because of his personal experience and expertise, he does a great deal of corporate planning and group-benefits coverage, with special emphasis on disability protection. He works with a wide range of clients but has a special affinity with business owners.

Peter is involved with Ducks Unlimited, Northern B.C. Friends of Children and the Forestry Expo charity fund raising. When not in the office he enjoys the outdoors, travelling, reading and spending time with his wife, Dawn, and their two children.

Peter may be reached by telephone at 250-564-7484 or by fax at 250-563-3281. His website is www.moneyconceptspg.bc.ca.

16

Dismantling the Myths of Financial Planning

By Cheryl Webb, CFP, RFP

*T*here are too many myths about personal financial planning and too many people believe them. Lack of financial education in the schools and inappropriate attitudes inherited from our parents and grandparents contribute to a lot of them. Contributing also is today's information glut—information overload really—from too many sources (some of them suspect, with axes to grind). Let's look critically at some of those myths.

MYTH:

Financial planning is only for the wealthy

Not true. Years ago financial planning was a privilege only the wealthy could indulge in because it was very expensive. A wealthy person could afford to call upon the expert services of specialized tax lawyers and accountants, a life underwriter, a health-insurance underwriter, mutual fund experts, tax- and estate-planning specialists, a bank advisor and so on. Today financial planning is very different, for two reasons: computers and the development of a new industry. The "miracle of the microchip" as Grant Sylvester calls it in his financial-planning book, *The Money Jar*, handles in minutes the formerly labour-intensive calculations that a battery of accountants, book-keepers, auditors and actuaries would have needed weeks to compile. Within a few hours a qualified, professional financial planner can develop a complete financial-planning strategy for middle- or even modest-income clients. The cost is negligible and may be handled in different ways.

At the same time, personal financial planning has developed as an industry—

one of the fastest growing in the country. Many people offer financial planning services but you should be careful to determine the most qualified among them. There are professional designations that, in part, qualify practitioners to work effectively on your behalf.

So, financial planning for even modest income-earners is affordable. It should be mandatory for most people.

MYTH:

I don't need a plan—my parents and grandparents didn't

That was then, this is now. Life is different. Financial planning by previous generations was a lot easier and almost invisible. The first step was to buy a house and pay for it. The next step was to put away a little money for a rainy day and/or retirement. The investment of choice was a GIC and you just drove around town and found the bank paying the highest rate. The, less money went a lot further, and besides, the value of that house surged disproportionately over the years.

Many retirees today might have a net worth of $250,000 (a home worth $100,000 to $150,000 and savings of $100,000). They expect that this along with their government benefits will see them through. But it's not likely to.

First, we are living longer. We will need a lot more retirement money than before to assure that it doesn't run out before we die.

Second, inflation is always with us and quietly undermines our ongoing purchasing power. The cost of living goes up every year but our fixed retirement income doesn't much, except for a small portion of indexed government pension. In fact, inflation as it affects the retired is often more than the official inflation Cost Price Index (CPI), because seniors use many different products and services than those the CPI officially includes. A 1990 study found that while the official inflation rate was 6%, the real inflation rate for retired people was 9% to 50% higher.

People often tell me that they had plenty of money when they first retired but they now are down to their last $100,000. They want to know how to make it last the rest of their lives. After we do our best for them, they frequently tell us that if we had met when they first retired they'd be a lot better off today. It's never too late to do something, but it is sometimes too late to do as much as we would like.

Everybody needs to plan in our age of self-reliance. Things have changed, in a big way. That's why the financial planning industry has grown at such a rapid pace.

MYTH:
Almost anybody in the financial services industry can be a planner

No. The financial services industry has grown so quickly that its terminology and formal qualifications are still in flux. As a result, many people in the industry, be they accountants or stockbrokers or bank personnel, consider themselves planners when they are not. They may be expert in one area of planning, but they do not necessarily have the overall planning expertise that you need. And not every qualified planner is even the right one for you; personalities must mesh. You have to find an effective planner with whom you are comfortable.

Not long ago I met with a retired couple. George was age 72 and Maria was 68. They had been to another financial planner who had set up an investment portfolio for them. Maria had since acquired more money to invest and wanted a second opinion. My colleagues and I had a series of meetings with them to determine their personal and financial goals, their risk tolerance, their retirement plan and their estate plan. The investments the first planner suggested did not reflect their level of risk tolerance and needed to be changed. We discovered they had not brought their wills up to date and that they should consider establishing a testamentary trust for income-splitting purposes. They also needed to insure their RRIFs against estate-tax liability because they wished to leave as much as possible to their beneficiaries.

Their former planner had done part of the job—the investments—though not all of these were appropriate. The tax and estate planning were neglected. Maria and George received a graphic lesson that all financial planners are not equal. After we finished, George told us, "We have met with a lot of different planners and you are the only one who has been able to answer all of our questions without referring back to a book."

So, how do you find the right planner?
First, you need somebody you are comfortable working with because planning is a process that never ends. It is not a single event and you should

expect to have a long-lasting relationship with whomever you choose.

Second, you need somebody who has the knowledge, the experience and preferably formal planning credentials.

You start by getting some referrals from friends or business associates. Then you interview some of the planners who seem to be the best for you, to determine whether you likely could have a comfortable working relationship with each other over time.

What credentials are you looking for?
There are a number of financial-planning designations that signify a practitioner's experience and continuing development through ongoing study. But the field is still somewhat fragmented and a single standard does not exist. In 1995 the industry attempted to bring most of the major players together through the Financial Planners Standards Council of Canada to provide a single Certified Financial Planner (CFP) designation. Since then some participating organizations have withdrawn and the single industry standard remains elusive, though desirable.

The Canadian Association of Financial Planners offers the Registered Financial Planner (RFP) designation, considered the premium designation available. The Canadian Association of Insurance and Financial Advisors offers the Chartered Life Underwriter (CLU) and The Chartered Financial Consultant (CH.F.C.) designations. To maintain these designations a planner must obtain a required number of ongoing educational credits each year.

MYTH:
There is so much planning information available, you can do it yourself

---

Forget it. A decade ago when I became a professional financial planner, it was a fairly new calling and few people knew what it was all about. Today you can't pick up a newspaper or magazine without reading about it or watch television without seeing a commercial about life insurance or mutual funds. Bookstores have entire sections devoted to business, investment, tax and money management.

You'd think that all this information would make it easy to become your own financial planner. On the contrary. Much of it is complicated and sophisticated—and contradictory—and the result often is confusion. I call this *information paralysis.* One of the main functions of a financial planner is to help you sort out the pertinent information for your individual circumstances. Even if you had the time (a lot of time if you're not an expert) and the knowledge, a planner's expertise is invaluable.

MYTH:

You have to earn a lot or have saved a lot before starting to plan

Nonsense. Many people believe this, but the earlier you start, the better off you'll be. You need a strategy to save effectively either for the short or long term. I define wealth as having enough money to do the things you want to do, when you want to do them, and knowing that there is enough to last your lifetime. Comprehensive financial planning is dedicated to achieving that and is not a get-rich-quick process; it is a well-developed plan of saving a little over a long time, which paves the road to wealth. As Grant Sylvester wrote in *The Money Jar*, "You could spend your entire life from age 20 dishing out hamburgers, fries and milkshakes at McDonald's, and still end up financially secure. You'd just have to put aside $20 a week and in 35 years you'd have saved $1,135,296." That assumes you use an RRSP that earns an average 14.5%. Saving a further five years would almost double that total.

MYTH:

There isn't much I can do about taxes

Ridiculous. There is plenty you can do to reduce the tax you pay—and quite legally. It's important to understand what marginal tax rate you are paying

INCOME TAX BRACKETS IN ONTARIO

Total Income	Regular Income	Dividends	Capital Gains
Up to $30,000:	27%	7%	21%
$30,000–60,000:	43%	26%	33%
Beyond $60,000:	53%	36%	40%

Source: Revenue Canada

and what types of income you receive. Different types of income are taxed differently and often you have a choice of what kind of income to go after.

This said, it sometimes happens that tax-planning and investment strategies conflict. One investment may be advantageous from the tax perspective but the return from that particular investment may not allow you to reach your retirement or income goals.

The table on the previous page indicates that dividend income is the most tax efficient, but you have to weigh that against the return you need to meet your financial goals. Dividend income these days usually provides a 6% to 8% return; if you require 8% to 10% you may have to switch some of your portfolio to a capital-gain type of investment. A planner can be of great help with the tax aspect of investing.

MYTH:
Mutual funds are too risky

Not at all. Perhaps this attitude results from the notion that if you do nothing, you won't make a mistake and thus won't be risking anything. In fact, doing nothing is the biggest risk of all—taxes and inflation actually put you into reverse gear.

Many people define risk as the loss of their principal or capital. This is only partially right. The proper definition of risk is twofold:

♦ loss of capital
♦ loss of your capital's purchasing power

Regarding loss of capital, a reliable financial planner can measure your risk tolerance and tailor investments accordingly. That doesn't mean you will completely escape the stock market's inevitable ups and downs, but it does mean you likely won't lose sleep because of them. Apart from your risk tolerance, the degree of investment risk depends too, upon how many years you have left until you retire and need investment income. The longer the period, in general, the more risk you may take because you have a longer recovery time if things go bad for a while.

Regarding purchasing power, many people hearken back to the "good old days" when you could earn 12% interest from almost risk free GICs. Going back further to the early 1980s, interest yields were up to 19%. But was that better than today? Not at all. Taxes took half of those great returns away and a 12% inflation rate left you in the hole. You are better off today, even with

THE GOOD OLD DAYS—NO WAY!

	1981/82	*Today*
Interest rate	19%	5%
Minus taxes (at 50%)	9.5%	2.5%
Minus inflation	12%	1.5%
RESULT:	*(2.5%)*	*1.0%*

relatively low 5% GIC rates. The following table shows you why:

A 5% return usually is not enough for most people to build a comfortable retirement fund—or for those already retired and living on investment income. You need a higher return because taxes and inflation erode the purchasing power of your money, and you might have to encroach on your capital and risk running out of money in a few years. One way around that is to take more investment risk—likely resulting in a higher return—but make sure it is a controlled risk, in accordance with your risk tolerance and circumstances. That's where a planner can help you.

MYTH:
I'm too old to invest in mutual funds

Never. It's true that mutual funds are a long-term investment. Long term, however, is generally conceded to be five to 10 years. Even if you were 60 or 65 years old today, the right mutual funds can still be suitable. There is a large assortment to suit almost everybody's circumstances. Funds offer certain advantages, such as professional management, diversification poten-tial, possible tax-deferral, a history of returns as a guide and liquidity.

Remember, we are all living longer. The average 60-year-old Canadian will live to age 80 or 83, so you should be planning for a life expectancy of 90 or 95 to make sure that your money will last as long as you do. That's a 30- to 35-year time frame and that certainly qualifies as a long-term investment.

MYTH:

Why should I bother with estate planning?
When I'm gone, who cares (it's not my problem)

A lot of people care, and so should you. The term "estate planning" smacks of the wealthy and perhaps that's one reason some people swallow this myth. It's also because estate planning for the average income earner is a fairly recent phenomenon and thus not widely understood. What is particularly misunderstood is the effect of doing nothing: families and other beneficiaries have lost significant amounts of money because of poor or a lack of planning.

A financial plan will help a client understand the importance of estate planning. It doesn't have to be a big deal—it could simply be making sure the tax angles are covered; or making sure the client has an up-to-date will and powers of attorney.

If you die intestate (without a will) your assets may end up being distributed the way the government or courts think is fair, not the way you might have apportioned them. The only way you can be sure that your assets will be distributed the way you want them to, is to have a will. It's not costly to have one drawn up and you should not be without one.

You also need appropriate powers of attorney. Using these documents, you outline what should happen if you become incapacitated and unable to fulfil your responsibilities. You designate someone to make financial and/ or medical decisions for you if you are unable. Powers of attorney cease at your death and are replaced by the instructions in your will.

Revenue Canada is patient, but it gets you in the end

Tax considerations are a part of estate planning. Many people who try everything to reduce their yearly tax bite sometimes completely ignore what will (probably) be the biggest tax bill they or rather their estates will ever face. For instance, when you die Revenue Canada will grab 50% of your RRSP and/or RRIF (assuming there is enough to place you in the 50% bracket). In other words, the government is a 50% beneficiary in your estate.

This does not apply, of course, to a spouse inheriting. But when your spouse dies, Revenue Canada would get the first $100,000 from your RRIF or RRSP with a $200,000 balance in it, before your estate can be split among your children.

Also, in your year of death, your portfolio usually is considered sold at market prices the day you died, and all capital gains are added to the income of that last year. If you have any estate at all, that should push the tax bracket to the top.

If you worked hard all of your life with the idea of making the government a major beneficiary, you can forget about estate planning. If that idea appalls you as it does most people, your planner can suggest techniques and ap-proaches that can help you reduce the tax bite. That's part of their job and it will not necessarily cost you anything.

MYTH:
Planning, investing and managing money is men's work

Absurd, of course. Women outlive their male partners on average by 10 to 14 years so they'd better learn how to handle savings, investments and assets. This kind of shared knowledge too, can add to the quality of their partnership over the years.

Many years ago I saw a moving and compelling trust company television commercial. It was only shown for a couple of months but it really got the point across that it is foolish to leave yourself financially vulnerable at a time when your are most emotionally vulnerable. It opened with a distraught woman behind a huge desk in what obviously was a man's book-lined study or office. The only light was on the desk, shining pointedly on a confusing mass of papers.

The woman, pushing her fingers distractedly through her hair, shook her head as she surveyed the overwhelming task ahead of her. After a second she mused to herself something like, "Bill, you always said there was lots of time to explain this to me—the difference between GICs, stocks and bonds . . ."

A woman should learn about money management as early as possible, but it's never too late (as the next chapter in this book will demonstrate). A professional financial planner is a great help with this process because a planner doesn't plan in a vacuum: the client is and always must be a full partner in the process.

MYTH:
Financial planning is a one-time event

Not in the least. Financial planning is a process, not an event. Overall it incorporates tax, estate and retirement planning along with investment strategy. You (and your planner) start by taking a look at where you are today, what you want to have happen down the road (your goals) and then look at changes you can make to improve your current and future lifestyles. This planning takes time and, once done, client and planner should continue to meet to review the client's changing needs.

We like to think of financial planning as a six-step process as this graphic indicates:

Here is a brief description of each step:

1. Acquire a personal financial planner. We have discussed this earlier in the chapter.

2. Assemble data. Your planner needs to develop a net worth statement, cash flow analysis, a retirement and an estate plan for you. You will need to provide your planner with statements from all of your savings accounts and investments; a list of GICs, RRSPs, RRIFs and CSBs; current mortgage status; loans/line of credit; credit cards; group benefit booklet from employment; life insurance policies; copy of will and powers of attorney; and most recent income-tax returns.

3. Set goals. This is often the most difficult part of planning–your planner will help. Where do you want to be in five or 10 or 20 years? Some relatively simple goals are to save for children's education, or a holiday or the purchase of a cottage. You may wish to reduce your yearly tax hit. An awkward retirement-goal decision can be whether to live well during your mature years or leave the maximum possible to children (if you can't do both).

4. Evaluate needs. How much money will you need to send children to college or university in 15 years? How much do you need to save for retirement in 20 years? How much life insurance do you need and what kind? Do you need disability insurance when you are already covered at work? The answers to these and other questions allow your planner to develop a strategy that suits your individual needs.

5. Write Plan. At this stage your planner incorporates the information you supplied and strategies related to your income, current lifestyle, your goals and your comfort level, into a written personal financial plan. This will be the road map to your financial peace of mind. It will lay out what to do and when to do it. You will understand what you need to do to stay on target.

6. Implement plan. At this point you need to implement your financial plan or you have wasted your time and energy. If you want to improve your circumstances you likely will have to change the way you have been doing things. Your plan and your planner will help you make the necessary changes. If you weren't satisfied with your financial situation and what it looked like down the line, you can't keep doing the same things. Change is never easy but you have a professional planner to help you.

The process does not stop here

Your personal circumstances are likely to change over the course of a year as will the economy and the rules and regulations in the financial services industry. There will be new financial products and services that could help you attain your goals. For this reason you must stay in touch with your planner. At the very least you should expect an annual review so your planner can recommend changes needed to fine-tune your plan and keep it on target.

There is never a better time than right now

I hope this chapter helps dispel some of the financial planning myths you might have subscribed to. Planning is an idea whose time has arrived. Even if you were inclined to do your own planning, you probably don't have the time—or the expertise in the various categories you need. In other aspects of life you use professionals: a mechanic for your car; a doctor for your health; an accountant for tax returns; and a lawyer to help you buy a house and prepare your will. You wouldn't think of trying to do these things on your own. Financial planning is no different and is just as important. Mistakes can be expensive and may have a serious impact on your future. Don't wait; find a financial planner today and get planning.

CHERYL WEBB has been providing financial planning advice and insurance services for clients since 1988. A Certified Financial Planner (CFP) and a Registered Financial Planner (RFP), she owns and manages a Money Concepts financial planning centre in Midland, Ontario.

Among her honours and awards, Cheryl has been both a Money Concepts President's Club and Chairman's Club qualifier since 1991. She was elected to the Money Concepts regional advisory council from 1993 to 1997. Her goal is "to function as a partner to help clients achieve a comfortable lifestyle today while providing for tomorrow."

She focuses her financial planning practice on retirement, estate and tax planning for relatively-high-net-worth individuals, business owners and retirees.

Cheryl may be reached by telephone at 705-527-0144 and by fax at 705-527-0932.

17

What's a Woman to Do?

Rebecca was 67 years old.
She had never written a cheque.   *By Beverly Young, CFP*
She had no idea of their financial situation.
She didn't know what to do.

*I*t sounds hard to believe in this day and age, yet this was an actual scenario that unfolded the day Lynn walked into my Trenton, Ontario, office for her semi-annual financial plan review. She seemed tense and distracted, not her usual happy self. It wasn't long before she told me what was on her mind.

"You probably don't know, but my dad had a stroke six months ago. He's not getting any better. Mom's not coping well. I've heard of the sandwich generation," she mused with tears in her eyes, "but now I really know what it means. Do you think you could spend some time with Mom and me, to get things sorted out?"

Mom—Rebecca Brown—was 67 years old. Her husband, William, was 71, and until he suffered a stroke, he very ably managed their finances. However, he now was in a nursing home with considerable loss of physical and mental faculties. Rebecca had never written a cheque. She had no idea of their financial situation. She didn't know what to do. She had always assumed that her husband would be there to take care of her. Suddenly, she was thrown into an unfamiliar and uncomfortable situation.

William Brown had worked for the local branch of a large Canadian corporation for 35 years. He received a good monthly pension as well as Canada Pension Plan and Old Age Security cheques. Also, he had astutely purchased an annuity a few years previous. It paid a good monthly income and was a joint annuity so the income would continue to Rebecca for as long as she lived if something happened to him.

Rebecca had relied on William to take care of all aspects of their finances.

They had always lived in a small, rented apartment above a downtown store and they spent their summers at their cottage that they loved dearly. The Browns had three children. Peter, living hundreds of miles away in Windsor, Ont., was married and had two children in their early teens. Karen was a single mother living with her eight-year-old daughter a couple of hours away in Ottawa. Peter and Karen had busy lives and weren't particularly close to their parents; they visited only two or three times a year. My client, Lynn, was married with two teenaged children and lived in the same town as her parents, so most of the care-giving responsibilities fell to her.

A few days after Lynn's visit, I met Rebecca for the first time. She was short and plump with curly, grey hair and arrived carrying an old briefcase. She was hesitant and nervous. I'm sure she was wondering what she was getting herself into. I usually meet with new clients three times. The first meeting is to get acquainted and gather information about their assets, liabilities, cash flow and goals. During the second meeting I present their financial plan with my recommendations. These could include tactics like building a cash buffer or emergency fund, an insurance-needs analysis, plus an analysis of how much they need to accumulate through RRSPs. They incorporate strategies to fund their children's education, to accumulate a retirement fund and to maximize their current investments. I deal with retirement issues that include maximizing income, minimizing taxes and passing an estate efficiently to heirs. At the third meeting we take action on implementing the recommendations they choose to accept.

I immediately foresaw six or seven meetings instead of the usual three

Rebecca opened her briefcase, pulled out a plastic bag filled with statements, and I immediately foresaw six or seven meetings instead of the usual three. Our first task was to discover the Browns' current financial situation. Rebecca came several successive Thursdays, each time with another plastic grocery bag filled with bankbooks and statements, some long expired and some current. We painstakingly sorted through each pile and my assistant, Dale, compiled from them a summary of the Browns' investments. We discovered the portfolio consisted of $530,000 invested in a combination of RRSP and non-RRSP guaranteed investment certificates (GICs) at their local bank, maturing at various times during the next four years.

We've never had a new car. I've always fancied a new car. Do you think I can afford one?

I'll never forget the look on Rebecca's face when she saw her portfolio statement for the first time with all the assets listed. It took a few minutes for the numbers to sink in, then very hesitantly she asked, "Are you sure this is right? I had no idea that William had saved this much." She paused. "I never thought we had any money. I always had to pinch pennies and ask William for money for extras. We bought all our clothes at the bargain stores. We've never had a new car. I've always fancied a new car. Do you think I can afford one?" Of course the answer was, "Yes, Rebecca, I think you can afford a new car." Before our next meeting began, she pulled me outside to look at her new blue sedan that she insisted on driving to take Lynn and me to lunch!

Our next task was to articulate Rebecca's goals. They were few: take a cruise, maintain an adequate monthly income and leave an inheritance to her children. She also wanted to give some money now to her children and other relatives, "while I'm still here to see them enjoy it."

To meet those goals we created a plan to diversify the Browns' investments, preserve their capital and decrease taxes and eventual probate fees. Rebecca had a lot to learn. We started with the basics of investing and progressed to the involved business of estate planning. She was an eager pupil and quite proud of her ability to grasp this new knowledge. More than once she arrived for our meeting waving a new statement and saying, "Look, I found another one."

Peter suggested that Rebecca use a trust company

At a family get-together during one of his rare trips home, Peter began to pay more attention to his mother's finances, asking more and more questions. He suggested to Rebecca that she consider having a trust company manage everything for her. Peter felt she was too old to learn how to manage not only her investments but also the day-to-day bills that she had always been sheltered from. He actually arranged for a meeting with a trust officer during his visit. Rebecca was in quite a huff afterwards and blurted out, "Why is

Peter all of a sudden so interested in what's going on? And why would I pay a trust company all that money for something you and I can do?"

Rebecca had no will. I strongly suggested she needed one

William had made a will leaving everything to Rebecca. However, Rebecca had no will. I strongly suggested that she needed one, if for no other reason than when you die without one, the government may, in essence, make one for you. That's not the best choice for those of us who have worked hard to accumulate assets and want to pass on our property and personal possessions as we see fit, because the government directive may well not coincide with our wishes. Rebecca could make a holograph (handwritten) will that would be perfectly legal. However, I always recommend using a lawyer. It's one of the best $200 investments you could make. It ensures that your wishes are followed, every possibility is covered and that there are no ambiguities to argue over. Rebecca opted for a lawyer who encouraged her to be very specific about her wishes so there would be no misunderstandings among the children when she was gone. Rebecca retorted indignantly, "Oh, my children would never be like that." Nevertheless, she followed his advice.

A POA covers both personal care and financial responsibility

The lawyer also prepared a power of attorney to cover the possibility that Rebecca might become incapacitated and unable to make her own decisions. The POA gave her children the power to make decisions and to act on her behalf. It covered both personal care and financial responsibility.

We then had a major financial issue to address. When I explained to Rebecca that their assets at the bank were only insured under the Canadian Deposit Insurance Corporation (CDIC) up to $60,000 for each of their RRSPs and bank accounts, she was incredulous. "That can't be right," she said. "Why didn't William know that? He should have known that. Why did he leave it all in one place?" We dealt with the problem by splitting off insurable amounts of some of their assets into other financial institutions.

As the Browns' GICs gradually matured we started diversifying their holdings. Our approach was conservative. Since they had already accumulated

Diversification means more than having GICs in different banks

wealth, our goal now was to preserve capital, obtain reasonable growth to offset inflation and to minimize taxes and probate fees. Rebecca quickly grasped the investment basics and chuckled when I explained to her that diversification meant far more than having your GICs in three different banks. In Rebecca's case achieving adequate diversification meant looking at investments that neither she nor William had ever used before. Some of their soon-to-mature GICs were five years old and carried 12% interest. Five years later. interest rates were about 5%. If you were in a 50% tax bracket and inflation was 2%, a new, 5% GIC would give the Browns a real return of only half of 1%–hardly enough to provide even modest growth beyond a basic inflation protection.

We combined segregated funds and GICs

We decided on a combination of segregated funds and GICs with life insurance companies for most of the RRSPs. A segregated fund is the life insurance industry's version of a mutual fund. However, segregated funds have some useful features that standard funds do not, such as:

♦ creditor protection in the case of bankruptcy
♦ a death benefit and maturity guarantee of 75% to 100% of the original amount, which provides reassurance while allowing the investor to benefit from long-term market performance
♦ named beneficiaries that allow assets to bypass probate

These last two were the most important for Rebecca. The guarantees were important to offset downturns in the stock markets. While the RRSPs would still be taxable upon Rebecca's death, the benefit of RRSPs bypassing probate directly to a named beneficiary would save money on probate fees. The government levies probate fees before allowing a will to be processed and the assets distributed. In Ontario, probate fees are $5 per thousand on the first $50,000 of assets subject to probate, and $15 per thousand on the remainder. Probate fees on the Browns' investments alone would be $7,450. Add at least another $1,500 fee for the cottage and other assets, and Rebecca realized that this was a strategy the Browns couldn't afford to pass up.

William had done a good job of accumulating savings and building spousal RRSPs for Rebecca. However, he had taken little advantage of other income-splitting strategies. It's usually advantageous to split retirement income as evenly as possible between spouses to minimize the taxes payable. Since Rebecca had never worked outside the home and therefore had no company pension or CPP income, it made sense to split William's CPP benefit between the two of them. But before we could do that, William passed away, and the picture changed. Instead of applying to split CPP, we completed the papers so Rebecca could receive her spousal CPP benefit.

Systematic withdrawal plan helped replace income

William's pension continued for Rebecca but, like most plans, the survivor's benefit was reduced to 60% of the former total—quite a pay cut. Now we had to increase Rebecca's monthly income to compensate for this drop. We did this by converting some of her non-registered (non-RRSP) funds into a systematic withdrawal plan (SWIP) and converting some of her RRSPs into RRIFs since she was almost 69, the mandatory age for maturing RRSPs.

A SWIP may reduce taxes

A SWIP consists of a lump-sum deposit or purchase. In Rebecca's case we split the investment between a dividend mutual fund and an international fund. We invested $100,000 and set it up to pay out 8% ($666) each month as income. If the fund earns a yield of 10% and you withdraw 8%, the original investment will increase by 2 % annually. I recommended leaving in the fund anything beyond the 8% return, so it would grow. That would give Rebecca the option of giving herself a raise every few years. There can be an added advantage to a SWIP: the income you receive is usually a combination of capital gains and dividends (depending on the types of funds in the SWIP), both of which, in Rebecca's case, were taxed at a lower rate than the purely interest income from GICs she had received before.

To top up her monthly income beyond the $666 to near where it was before the pension was cut back, we used income from the RRIFs. You are obliged by law to redeem a specified minimum amount from a RRIF each year, although you can take more than the minimum if you want. Once Rebecca saw the monthly payments from the SWIP and RRIFs being deposited into her bank account, she started to relax somewhat.

She offset tax liability with life insurance

We now started to consider the tax implications of Rebecca's eventual death. Since her situation had changed when William died, she decided to review her will with her lawyer. At his death, their RRSPs transferred directly to Rebecca as surviving spouse, with no tax liability. However, when she passes away, RRSP assets would be treated as being matured, or cashed in, and thus taxable. This would mean that half Rebecca's RRSPs would go towards paying taxes. One way around such a substantial liability can be a life insurance policy with the proceeds providing a non-taxable cash payment to help offset taxes, probate and funeral expenses. Life insurance can be a cost-effective way of leaving an estate to your heirs, which Rebecca wanted to do. The policy would have named beneficiaries, not including her estate. This would help reduce probate fees. To pay for the monthly premium payment, we would use income from her RRIFs. At the age of 67, however, Rebecca needed a medical examination to qualify for insurance. Unfortunately, her test results led the company to deny coverage. So, we had to look at different options to preserve her estate.

To maximize an estate, minimize probate fees

You can help preserve an estate by reducing potential probate and taxes, using methods such as setting up joint ownership of assets, designating beneficiaries or even just giving some of it away in advance. We decided on a combination of approaches. First, Rebecca made Lynn a joint owner of her bank accounts. Next, she divided a portion of her non-RRSP funds into three diversified mutual-fund portfolios, each owned jointly with one of her children. At her death these assets would transfer directly to the joint owner and not be subject to probate. Then she transferred other of her non-RRSP reserves into life insurance company (segregated) investments with named beneficiaries. This also would be outside probate.

In keeping with Rebecca's wanting "to get things in order," she decided to transfer her beloved cottage to the three children jointly. By doing so, Rebecca gave up ownership but luckily the Browns had taken advantage of their capital-gains exemption on the cottage before the government scrapped this benefit, so there was minimal tax liability. The children were now jointly responsible for maintenance, taxes and capital gains on the cottage.

Three years after I started working with Rebecca, I attended her 70th birthday party and met all the relatives I had only heard about before. Unfortunately, her health was failing, so she decided to enjoy some of her money while she could. She took her two daughters on a cruise, and escorted the four oldest grandchildren to Disney World. She gave a small sum of money to each of her children and grandchildren. She also helped her favourite niece and nephew with some of their university tuition costs, and made a donation to her church.

I watched her enjoy some rewards for those hard, earlier years of scrimping and saving

Soon though, she had to accept the fact that she could no longer live on her own. She gave up her apartment and moved in with Lynn and her family. Rebecca paid for an addition to Lynn's small house so there was enough space for her. As she became weaker, I watched Peter and Karen become more and more involved with Rebecca and more and more interested in her assets. They began to question decisions that Rebecca, Lynn and I had made jointly over the previous three years, years when Peter and Karen had been too busy with their own lives to have much time for their parents. They started to demand explanations for each of Rebecca's financial decisions: "Why did you choose that investment? What did you do with the money from the GIC you cashed? Who is the beneficiary? What was that money used for?" I attended a few joint meetings with Rebecca, Lynn, Peter and Karen to explain the changes we had made and the rationale behind each decision. Sometimes Rebecca patiently answered their questions about what she had done. Sometimes she chose to ignore them. Sometimes, I was caught in the middle. My job as Rebecca's financial planner was to redeem funds when she asked me to, as tax efficiently as possible. What she did with her money was her affair. One day she became so fed up with Peter's interference, that she told him it was none of his business and sent him home.

Eventually, Rebecca became bedridden and was confused at times. Yet she still had moments of clarity where her sharp wit would show itself with an edge of caustic sarcasm. She became very irritable and touchy when Karen or Peter probed too much. Rebecca died almost a year ago. I'd like to think that her last few years were happy ones, and I believe they were. I watched her enjoy some rewards for those hard, earlier years of scrimping and saving. I took pleasure from sharing in her financial education and seeing her confidence grow to the point where she could make capable decisions about her finances and delighted in doing so.

Her beloved cottage was sold the following spring. Lynn wanted to keep the cottage in the family for the grandchildren, but Rebecca's three children couldn't agree on how to split the costs of upkeep. They spent more time bickering about it than they did enjoying the place. Finally, Lynn gave in to the wishes of the other two mainly because she did not want to contend with the problems that were evolving. Rebecca's remaining assets were divided as her will dictated. Her three children are now estranged, with Peter and Karen insinuating that Lynn took some of her mother's money.

Rebecca and William had been "depression babies." They had grown up imbued with the necessity of frugality and had always found money a difficult topic to discuss with each other, let alone with their children. Perhaps if the communication channels had been more open through the years, the conflicts and suspicion that arose among Peter, Karen and Lynn could have been avoided.

BEVERLY YOUNG is president of Money Concepts, Quinte/Prince Edward district in Ontario. Her goal is to help clients to secure their financial independence by combining the Money Concepts corporate tradition of providing individual, objective, financial advice with the personal characteristics of integrity, professionalism and trust.

Bev is rooted in her community and will be there for many years. She is a long-time resident of the Quinte area and is actively involved in the Business & Professional Women's Club. She is also active in local co-op education programs with Loyalist College and area high schools. Bev began her professional life as a registered nurse and brings to her business life a deep sense of caring for individuals and their needs. She believes that truly listening is the best way to understand clients' financial goals. She shares her knowledge by contributing articles to local newspapers as well as by organizing money-management educational seminars.

She has received a local media Reader's Choice award for Favourite Financial Planner for the past three years. Her professional standards and performance have consistently earned her membership in Money Concepts President's Club and Chairman's Club. She also has earned her Certified Financial Planner (CFP) designation and she is a member of The Canadian Association of Financial Planners.

Bev may be reached at her Money Concepts office by telephone at 613-392-4540 in Trenton or 613-475 5678 in Brighton, and by fax at 613-392-4554.

18

How to Get the Most out of Your Financial Planner

By Jim Young, CA

*T*he talk around the office these days is how well Harry's investments are doing and what a great financial planner he must have. A few years ago most of the others in the office started an RRSP with the bank but you're not really sure where it is invested. "It's an RRSP. What else do you need to know?" You started it because the boss matched our contribution, and besides, everybody was getting involved.

That was a few years ago. Today there is a big retirement party for Harry. He's only age 58. How on earth did he manage it? After all, he is a salesman and has never had top-management income to play with.

You corner Harry at the party and ask him the BIG QUESTION: "How can you afford to retire at 58?" He likes to talk, and 20 minutes later you have the name and phone number of his financial planner, Jim. The next day, you call Jim and mention Harry's name and praises. You would also like to retire at age 58 you tell Jim, and you make an appointment. What now, you suddenly realize, what do you do to prepare for a meeting like this? You've never talked to a financial planner before.

Preparation is the key to effective planning

There has been a great deal written about how to find and choose a financial planner. But there's not much material around telling you how to get the most from the one you choose, and how to evaluate that person and his or her qualifications and capabilities. How can you ensure planners meet your needs, not just theirs? How do you prepare for a meeting, especially the first one? What do you take along with you to the appointment?

There is a fair amount you can do to prepare for that first meeting and subsequent ones with your financial planner so you can get the most for your time. I suggest a three-stage approach:

1. preparing for the first meeting
2. preparing for subsequent visits
3. the relationship with your planner

THE FIRST MEETING

You will spend more time preparing for the initial planning meeting than any other. The better you are prepared the more efficiently you will use your time. If you know in advance some of the questions the planner will ask of you, you will be better able to judge a planner's capability. Go into that meeting with some questions of your own and with some knowledge of the planning process so you won't be surprised. The more you know in advance, the better able you'll be to judge a planner's approach.

What can you expect a planner to do for you?

♦ They will work with you and guide you through the planning process, but not do all the work and provide all the needed information; you have to do your part.

♦ They will gather financial and personal information from you, which will help identify your needs, problems and opportunities—problems are opportunities waiting to happen.

♦ They will establish goals and set realistic priorities, again in conjunction with you.

♦ Finally, they will develop strategies to implement and monitor a financial plan that they will draw up for you.

What is the financial planning process?

There are six basic steps in the planning process:
1. *gathering information from the client*
2. *determining a client's concerns and needs*
3. *establishing financial objectives*

4.   *Creating strategies to meet the objectives*
5.   *Implementing the plan*
6.   *Monitoring the progress of the plan*

What constitutes a financial plan?

A general financial plan will consist of these:
- *statement of net worth*
- *statement of income and expenses*
- *retirement plan*
- *education plan*
- *insurance-needs analysis*
- *summary and recommendations*

A good planner will talk about change

One of the most important roles a planner performs is to help establish your concerns, problems and needs and goals. Think about these things before the first meeting. Usually, an objective assessment of your problems, needs and goals will require change—change, that is, on your part. Why is that? It's because you will probably have to change your financial arrangements, if you have any; otherwise you wouldn't need a planner. Understand, however, a planner will not, and cannot, change *you*. You will have to change yourself. They say that there are only three ways to change a person:
1. Brain surgery
2. Radical psychotherapy
3. Religious conversion

I don't know many financial planners qualified to handle any of those fields.

You can, however, change some of your own attitudes and habits. It's a multi-step process:

♦ **Awareness.** First you must be aware that there is a problem. (You might, for instance, become aware of a problem if somebody, without prompting, gives you a bottle of mouthwash.)

♦ **Understanding.** You must get a grasp of the problem—and the consequences of doing nothing. (Social ostracism, perhaps.)

♦ **Concern.** You must become concerned. (If you do not care about having bad breath, you will never do anything about it.)

♦ **Dissatisfaction.** Then you must become dissatisfied. (If you are not, you won't be motivated to change.)

♦ **Action.** If you have gone through the four previous stages, you will likely want to take action and make changes.

The key is to know that *you* will have to enact changes *yourself* to secure your financial future. Your financial planner will be your coach, your support. You will not need brain surgery or radical psychotherapy.

One person's problem is another's opportunity

A typical example of a person with a financial problem: you may be age 40 and have saved little for retirement. The future looks bleak. What to do? If you've gone through the stages above, you turn the problem into an opportunity. You set up a savings plan of $500 per month, designed to return a yield of 10%. At age 65 you will have a nest egg of $725,000. This will produce an annual income of about $70,000.

Look at problems positively and turn them into opportunities. Be creative.

Establishing your concerns, problems and needs

I mentioned earlier concerns, problems, needs and goals. You must establish these clearly so your planner can identify opportunities and develop strategies for your financial plan. How do you do this? You work with your planner. Good planners will spend more of their time and energy on this area of planning than any other.

It all starts during the first information-gathering meeting. Your planner should ask you a lot of questions. Some of these will help determine your current financial status. Many, however, should be open-ended questions that bring out your feelings and concerns. Some examples:

♦ How did you feel about that?

♦ When did you determine that?

♦ What are your concerns in this area?

- What do you mean?
- Where did you get that information from?
- Why do you say that?

Not all planners are good at this, since it involves a holistic approach to financial planning. Finding out what people are feeling is not easy. Determining concerns and problems is not a cakewalk. Many planners expend energy (and your time) trying to impress you with their knowledge of product, tax laws and computer expertise. They talk about the great support you will get from their organization and so on. *But what about you?* What's bothering you? What do you need now and in the future? Thoughtful answers will allow you and your planner to reshape problems into clear goals and objectives.

At the end of your first meeting, you and your planner should have established an agenda for subsequent visits. A typical agenda would contain:

1. a review of the draft financial plan the planner has drawn up— financial objectives along with strategies to meet these objectives

2. implementation strategies—recommendations and action plans

3. suggested financial products to implement the strategy

Before we talk about preparing for subsequent meetings, consider the following questionnaire and budget-calculation sheet plus suggestions about material to take along with you to that vital first meeting with your potential planner.

INITIAL MEETING PREPARATION

Answer these questions briefly, but after lengthy thought, before you go to the meeting (and take the answers with you):

- What does money mean to me?_____

_____

- What bothers me about my present financial situation?_____

_____

- Do I feel good about my financial future? Will I have enough money when I retire?_____

_____

♦ What would happen to my family and me if I should suddenly become permanently disabled? Or what if I were to die prematurely?_____

_____

♦ Can I afford to educate my children through university?_____

_____

For single people

♦ Would I be able to support myself if I became permanently disabled?_____
♦ To whom will I leave my estate?_____

_____

Each of these questions is designed to help make you aware of potential financial problems and to lead you to an understanding of the consequences of doing nothing. If you become concerned at this point and are dissatisfied with your present status, you are well on your way to changing—and improving—the situation.

Gather this information and prepare the following statements (Don't be intimidated; just do best you can.):

Statement of net worth
♦ List and place a value on your assets.
♦ List all your liabilities and amounts.
♦ Provide details of your RRSPs and loans.
Include all relevant paperwork and bring it along.

Statement of income and expenses
♦ What is your monthly take-home pay?_____
♦ What other income do you have?_____
♦ Allocate your monthly living costs/expenses as per the categories outlined on the following page.

HOUSING:	Rent/Mortgage/Interest	$
	Property taxes	$
	Heating	$
	Hydro	$
	Cable TV	$
	Telephone	$
	Property insurance	$
	Miscellaneous housing	$
	Recreational property	$
FAMILY:	Food and beverage	$
	Housekeeping	$
	Clothing	$
	Personal care	$
	Dependant care	$
	Medical and dental	$
TRANSPORTATION:	Vehicle payments(s)	$
	Gas/oil	$
	Repairs	$
	Insurance	$
	Parking/bus/cabs	$
	Licenses and permits	$
PERSONAL:	Life insurance	$
	Loan payments	$
	Vacations	$
	Clubs and dues	$
	Entertainment/hobbies	$
	Gifts	$
	Professional dues	$
	Charitable donations	$
	Pets and vets	$
	Pocket money	$

Retirement plans

◆   At what age would you like to retire?_____

◆   What is your current income?_____

◆   What is your current age?_____

◆   What is your life expectancy?_____

Education plans

Jot down the names of your children, their ages and the answers to the following questions :

	Name	Age
1.	_____	_____
2.	_____	_____
3.	_____	_____

◆   When will college begin?_____

◆   How many years in college?_____

◆   Note any educational funds you have:

Child	*Fund*	*$ Invested*
◆_____	_____	_____
◆_____	_____	_____
◆_____	_____	_____

Insurance needs analysis

Locate and bring to the meeting all current insurance policies including, life, disability and any group policies from work.

In general

If there are any financial matters you are particularly concerned about, e.g., your mortgage, bring the paperwork and details to the first meeting.

SUBSEQUENT MEETING PREPARATION

Before going to subsequent meetings with a planner, decide whether you really want to continue the process with that person or perhaps find somebody else to deal with. Positive answers to the following questions should indicate that you are feeling good about the process and the person. One or two negative responses suggest you should consider stopping and perhaps find somebody else you match up with more effectively.

Evaluating a planner
- ◆ Did you feel good about the first meeting?
- ◆ Did the planner ask you questions that brought out your concerns?
- ◆ Do you feel that the planner was working for you rather than for him or herself?
- ◆ Did you feel rushed or apprehensive?
- ◆ Did the planner answer your questions clearly? Did you understand the answers?
- ◆ Did the planner use a lot of jargon?
- ◆ Do you feel this person is competent?
- ◆ Would you recommend this person to your friends?

Make sure things happen

If you decide to continue, consider this: you and your financial planner can come up with the best financial plan ever developed. But if you simply toss it on a shelf, or table it, nothing will happen. You have to implement the plan and you have to review it regularly with your planner. If you don't, you could end up as one of the thousands who lived longer than the money they saved. You, the client, must be proactive and make sure things happen. The planner can't do it all.

If you don't review it, the plan won't do it

In grade nine I didn't do my homework unless I expected the teacher to review it. The fact that I knew math or English would be checked and graded the next day provided a terrific incentive to getting it done the night before. When I knew the teacher would not check it, I didn't do it. Financial planning is not all that different; it's essential to the success of your financial plan that you review it at least once a year or more. You and your planner should do (at least) this during a review:

- ◆ Reconsider the financial objectives and the investment results.

- ◆ Adjust investments, if needed.
- ◆ Review insurance needs.
- ◆ Analyze and deal with new concerns, tax changes, opportunities and circumstances.
- ◆ Update the financial plan, if necessary.

The annual financial plan review is not much different than a regular automobile check-up: it ensures the parts are well maintained and in good working order. Without doubt it is an essential part of achieving your financial goals.

YOUR RELATIONSHIP WITH YOUR PLANNER, AND YOUR RIGHTS

When you establish a working relationship with a planner, you should know what to expect, especially your rights as a client. These rights definitely should include:

- ◆ being treated in a courteous and professional manner no matter the size of your portfolio
- ◆ receiving accurate and professional advice
- ◆ being presented with strategies that are in *your* best interest, not those of the planner
- ◆ feeling free to telephone your planner when you need guidance, advice or are concerned
- ◆ expecting that your telephone calls will be returned
- ◆ having your plan and investment program reviewed on a regular schedule (agreed upon at your first meeting)
- ◆ full and open disclosure regarding the planner's methods of compensation and any potential conflicts of interest

Your planner has rights, too (two of them are pretty basic)

1. to be fairly compensated for professional advice and counselling
2. to receive referrals from you if they do a good job

When people always ask me, "How do you get paid?" every client gets the same answer. I review in detail how financial institutions compensate planners if and when they purchase investments to implement the client's plan. It's like a broker/client arrangement, or any agent receiving a commission for services rendered. I also tell them, "If I do a good job for you, you will refer your friends and acquaintances to me." That is part of my payment.

As far as referrals are concerned, consider it simply enlightened self-interest: if a planner receives enough referrals, he or she will not be spending a large percentage of time looking for new business—they will have more time to actively devote to your affairs.

Making things happen

Never forget that a financial planner, however expert, does not work alone. To make the process work, you must be an active partner. Perhaps a sports analogy would be useful: your planner is your coach and advisor. You still have to hit the ball. You will be more likely to make contact with that ball if you

- ◆ are proactive, not just passive and reactive
- ◆ think carefully about your concerns and needs
- ◆ make changes yourself, if necessary, about yourself
- ◆ objectively evaluate your planner and his or her performance
- ◆ make sure things happen (schedule reviews and ask questions)

If you do all this, your chances of striking out are a lot less, and, you may even hit a home run.

JIM YOUNG is the president of a Money Concepts office in Ottawa. Before he became a financial planner he was the managing partner of a large firm of chartered accountants.

He is a keen golfer and skier and enjoys making wine. Jim is active in the community and was president of the Ottawa Carleton Association for Persons with Developmental Disabilities, a member of the Hospital Advisory Board of the Carleton District Health Council and a member of the Student Advisory Board of Carleton University. He is founder and president of the Business Club at Algonquin College.

As a professional, Jim works in the areas of tax, retirement and estate planning. His focus tends to be on wealth creation and management, severance packages, single parents, retirees and baby boomers.

His business philosophy is simple: "I never do anything that is not in the best interests of my client." Jim keeps in close touch with his clients. This includes periodic reviews to assure that plans are current and are adapted to changing needs and circumstances.

Jim Young may be reached by telephone at 613-238-7818, and by fax at 613-238-8035.

19

Goal Setting: the (Hard) Core of Financial Planning

By Jan Fraser, CFP, M.Ed

*S*etting goals—personal and financial—is just one part of the financial planning process. But for many planners and many clients, it can be the toughest part—and the most critical to the success of the plan. Goals provide the foundation for your personal and financial plans. Goals give realistic meaning to your dreams. Thinking about your goals helps you set priorities, which in turn translate into a series of milestones you work toward, guided by a specific action plan. Goal setting is a process that enables you to live life fully in the present, inspired by goals that give purpose and meaning to your life. It can allow you to achieve that which you never would have believed possible.

That is why it is so important to have an understanding relationship with whoever is helping you assess your desires and set your priorities. You need to find someone who has the skill to help you articulate your (sometimes latent) core values. You need someone skilled in looking at ideas that have potential and at finding creative and useful ways to apply them. And you need someone who can take your goals and ideas and blend them into a comprehensive plan—a plan that lays out the milestones along with creative strategies to reach them, using your available resources to the fullest.

Setting goals is a softer, spongier process than laying out a zippy chart showing how your money can grow exponentially through the magic of compounding interest. It is relatively easy to demonstrate how a $50 per month investment can expand into a sizeable sum over 25 years. It takes a lot more energy and commitment to grapple with personal goals and aspirations and the priority-setting process.

It's possible—these people know

I recently received a postcard from a client in her late 40s. She had just moved to Mexico with her husband:

Buenos días Jan! Photo on this postcard is taken from mountain. We live in a condo at edge of town, and walk 1 mile to square every day. Lemons, limes, bananas, mandarins are outside our front door. Have only seen 2 clouds in the last 2 weeks—75 degrees again—ho hum. Everyone here calls it paradise, but it only has one golf course! We have no newspapers or English news to worry us, but we do now have a fax machine so if you need to reach us. . .

When I met this couple, they had accumulated mostly debt, not assets. But they had a spirit, a *joie de vivre*. Even in the face of serious health issues that precipitated major changes in their lives, they continued to explore ways to define and achieve their vision of the "good life." Based on the postcard and faxes, it sounds as if they have found their way.

Another couple I know is designing a retirement home in the South Pacific. They are going to be retiring early and plan to spend half the year out of Canada. They are even exploring business opportunities that could become part of their new life. When I met this couple, they had vacationed once in the South Pacific islands, but the thought of owning property and living there was the furthest thing from their minds. They will now be reaping the rewards of their money-management decisions (guided by their personal financial planner) as they retreat to their tropical paradise each year.

Are these people extraordinary? Not as most would see it. Are they wealthy? Not, perhaps, in monetary terms. Have they discovered the good life? Yes. It is said that you can't measure the most important things in life. While we really can't measure what we label the "good life," there are always indicators: financial well-being, freedom from personal debt, opportunities to travel, the ability to feed your kids or support a foster child.

You do need money, but how much you need and what constitutes *your* good life is something that you, not the media or marketers, should determine. You, not external forces like family, friends, journalists or even a financial advisor should decide what your values are and what you really want.

Most people aim too low rather than risk not achieving their goals. Fear of the unknown is one reason. Fear of the future is another. Fear of loss can contribute. Complacency holds many people back, as does an unwillingness to search for deeper meaning in their lives. Creative planning could do much for such cautious people and their families, but often they don't bother: they let circumstances manage them rather than making the effort to take matters into their own hands.

Perhaps that's why most people need a little help. There is no reason to think you have to do it all yourself. These days, competent, professional financial planning is available to everyone regardless of income. But it's important to choose the right planner to help you, particularly with setting goals and determining values.

Your relationship with your planner

A financial planner's job is to help you expand your horizons, aid you in clarifying the way you really want your life to be and perhaps even dare you to set goals that you might not normally think attainable. They can also help you to "get real" in relation to your particular reality. I have found with clients that getting real usually means focusing on what is truly important to them.

A planner, or third-party facilitator, should be non-judgmental and be able to devise imaginative solutions using the resources you have, limited or not. A planner should be inclined to take the initiative, to suggest not-so-ordinary approaches. They should help you explore beyond your comfort zone and show you how to live accordingly. They should help you enrich your life by engaging fully in a results-oriented, life-planning process.

Much has been written about the places to look for a planner. Once you have devised a shortlist, take your time deciding who is right for you. You must be comfortable with your planner; after all, it will be a long-term relationship, since periodic reviews are part of the planning process. You don't have to be embarrassed about switching to another advisor if you aren't getting along with the first one you choose.

But always remember: a personal advisor will provide only the external climate and the methods necessary for creating a successful financial and life plan. It will be up to you to provide the internal climate: a willingness and commitment to keep an open mind through every phase of the process, and to re-evaluate some of the opinions, attitudes and habits that you have cultivated throughout your life.

How to approach goal-setting

The essence of setting goals is digging deep within yourself to identify your core values and guiding principles. In simple terms, what is your purpose in life? What matters the most to you? What will enable you to live your life to the fullest? Clarifying values is an exercise in weighing and sifting, of examining the trade-offs in terms of your priorities. Most of us carry a lot of unnecessary baggage that sometimes obscures our view of what we really want. Clarifying values helps us drop that baggage at the left-luggage department so we can see more clearly.

Think about the weighing and sifting you would have to do to evaluate the following, for example:

♦   *What is more important to you:* no mortgage, or a new home and a new mortgage?

♦   *What is more important to you:* a new car every five years and money for a special trip, or a new car every three years and no money for a special trip?

♦   *What is more important to you:* money so your partner can return to college for further training, or investing for your retirement?

♦   *What is more important to you:* knowing that your family will receive $500,000 if you die on the way to work tomorrow, or having $500 each month accumulating in your retirement account?

♦   *What is more important to you:* renovations to a bathroom, or a trip to Disneyland?

♦   *What is more important to you:* lending money to your son for the down payment on his first home, or giving him the down payment?

♦   *What is more important to you:* retiring when you reach age 59, or working two more years so that you have an additional retirement income of $200 per month?

Some of these probably were easy for you to answer and some perhaps difficult to the point of discomfort. When you work through this process with your planner, you need to be honest. This method of forced choices helps you to get to the heart of your personal truths. Having to choose one or the other means you can't waffle or sit on the fence. You cut through much of the emotional clutter that complicates life's weightier decisions. This questioning and clarifying process enables you to commit to your priorities because you know they reflect your real values.

Remember, there are no correct answers other than what rings true for you. This process can be absolutely gut-wrenching if you find you have conflicting values or priorities or, more typically, your values conflict with those of your spouse or partner. Gut-wrenching or not, I guarantee that this process can and will be totally exciting if you trust it enough to let your real priorities and issues come to the surface. When we incorporate your true priorities into action plans, you will have a powerful tool that can almost automatically make future decisions for you—clear decisions that will advance you steadily toward your goals.

Look at the same thing from a different perspective

Your goal may be retirement at age 55. If you look at it a different way, you could see that retirement, in itself empty and simplistic, is not actually what you have in mind. Your goal really is to change gears, to use your days for different activities, to live without the pressure of having to go to work because of money needs. Perhaps you want to undertake community work. Perhaps you want to live in Greece and gaze at the sea, wander through olive groves and savour the aroma of Greek food in the kitchen or market. Creating such a goal, for example, engages your imagination and your daily efforts much more than stating simply that you will retire at age 55 and need $5,000 per month to be happy. Flesh out your real priorities with dramatic images and that will bring excitement to every minute you strive for them.

Setting goals is a quiet process, one of reworking, reframing. It doesn't occur during a 10- or 15-minute discussion with a planner. It is a process that you actively engage in when meeting with your financial planner, especially during the early stages of the relationship. It also occurs quietly during moments of reflection, when you're not even aware that you're thinking about life's opportunities and possibilities.

When a financial planner can come to understand what you really want, then he or she can apply professional knowledge and expertise to help you realize your dreams. People who think of their financial planners as number-crunching retailers of financial products are missing the boat. The value of the relationship lies in the planner's ability to help you discover your true desires, through clarifying your values and setting attainable goals, then devise and implement creative ways of achieving those goals.

Setting goals is a continuing activity, not a one-time task

Life (and financial planning) is an ongoing process, not a single event. It spans your lifetime. Sometimes circumstances change and then so will your goals and priorities. You might achieve one goal and find it gives rise to others. In a full and energetic life, goal setting is a dynamic, exciting, creative, energizing process. Often you have to make a great effort and dig deep to allow it to happen. It can be painful sometimes but worth it always.

Let's examine some ways to determine your values, goals and priorities— preferably before you see your financial planner. Be honest and let your ideas and issues rise to the surface. You might be surprised to discover that your real goals are not what you thought they were. Read over the items that follow. Think about them and jot down notes on separate sheets of paper that you can refer to when you see your planner. (I am indebted to Paul Stevens of Worklife Pty. Ltd. in Australia—web site: http://www.worklife.com.au/index.html—for much of the following material.)

It's helpful to acknowledge your personal strengths and reflect on how these qualities have been developed and shaped. Describe your special individuality or personality:

I am . . .

Your view of yourself, or self-image as it is frequently called, has been shaped by your experiences and, more specifically, your perception of your experiences—your successes and failures, triumphs and setbacks, good times and bad. Your self-image influences your every thought so it is worthwhile to freely respond to the following statements (again, on separate sheets of paper). The time and energy required for this self-exploration is a wise investment.

- ◆ Great moments in my life:
- ◆ I'm good at the following:
- ◆ I'm not good at the following:
- ◆ I would like to start doing:
- ◆ I would like to stop doing:
- ◆ Experiences I want to have:

- ◆ Talents and gifts that I would like to use:
- ◆ Places I want to spend time in, and why:
- ◆ People I want to spend time with, and why:

Now, identify a few statements about yourself that you believe you could change by applying what you have just answered. Then:

- ◆ describe five very good experiences that you've had.
- ◆ write about your five worst experiences.

Consider each of the experiences you described and write down what it is about the experience that you value. Concentrate on one at a time. For example, some of these qualities may come to mind: *security, influence, helpfulness, freedom, family life, tenacity, friendship, steadfastness, kindness, order, recognition, wealth, workmanship, new experiences.*

Based on your answers above, write down the three values most important to you:

1.
2.
3.

Imagine yourself five years from now. Write a detailed description of a typical day that would include many aspects of life that you desire for yourself.

Think about the specific projects or activities that you wanted to accomplish over the past five years, but which you postponed. Describe why you postponed each. What need(s) would have been fulfilled had you carried out the activity? Which if any of these projects or activities are still important to you? Re-evaluate the reasons for postponing. Did you defer or procrastinate because it was inconsistent with your values? Do you still need to put them off? If this project or activity is still relevant, assign a rating of importance, number one being most important. Consider how each relates to a personal goal that you want to achieve.

Before you move on to actual goal setting and commitment to specific objectives, look back over your notes and try to find patterns or recurring themes in your life. Think about what you want to achieve. Write down four or five broad goal statements, for example, *I want to achieve and maintain balance between my work life and my family life.*

Take each goal statement and answer the following:

◆ How high a priority do you attach to this goal? (Use whatever ranking system works for you: high-medium-low, A-B-C, 1-2-3.)

◆ Does this goal reflect your core values that you've now clarified?

◆ What internal factors, for example, self-image, attitudes, desires, will affect your ability to achieve this goal?

◆ What obstacles, if any, do you need to overcome?

◆ What will be the consequences if you don't achieve this goal?

◆ To what length are you prepared to go to achieve this goal?

Move from the general to the specific

From these broader life goals, identify specific objectives. At this point you need to build objectives that are S M A R T: Specific, Measurable, Achievable, Realistic and Truthful. You will find that the more specific you are, the more energized and focused you will become. Carry out the following audit of your objectives and revamp where needed:

◆ Does each specific objective start with the word "to" followed by an action word?

◆ Does each produce a single key result when achieved?

◆ Does each specify a target date for its achievement?

◆ Does each specify "what," "when," "why" and "how"?

◆ Is each tough and demanding but also realistic and attainable?

◆ Will the result justify the time, emotion and resources you will need to achieve it?

◆ Have you defined the goal(s) each objective will address?

◆ Have you identified at least two possible objectives for each goal?

◆ If you are working through this process without the assistance of a facilitator or planner, have you tested your planned goals and objectives with other people whose advice you value?

◆ Have you prepared (by yourself or with a planner) a plan of action to follow when you are confident that each objective will be taking you in the direction you want to travel (goals and dreams)? Identify the milestones, significant markers or checkpoints that you will use to measure your progress along the way. Make sure that you remember to celebrate your achievements as each milestone is reached.

Today's decisions determine tomorrow's life

We are living in one of the most challenging epochs of change human beings have ever faced. We can do things today that few of us would have dreamt possible a few short months ago. What will tomorrow look like? More importantly, what do you want your tomorrow to be? Much will depend on what you do today. We create our tomorrows by the decisions we make today. We don't live tomorrow or yesterday—we only live today. The present, albeit a moving target, is the only real time we have. By undertaking a comprehensive goal-setting process, in conjunction with your financial planner, you can enjoy an exciting today and a fulfilling and comfortable tomorrow.

JAN FRASER brought Money Concepts to Manitoba in 1987 when she established the first Money Concepts Financial Planning Centre in Winnipeg. Jan brings particular skill in helping people articulate and align their goals with their values, talents and resources. She has a keen grasp of the forces shaping the domestic and global economy, and a broad knowledge of global markets, tax-advantaged investment strategies and financial products. This enables her to build creative financial strategies that produce tangible results for her clients.

Showing a seasoned understanding of the needs of successful people, Jan's approach holds long-term growth, risk management and wealth creation for the generations to come as important elements of a successful financial plan

Jan's client base includes people from all walks of life, including dual-income couples, women and retirees. She is particularly interested in working with people to implement tax-efficient strategies for intergenerational wealth transfer and charitable giving.

Prior to Money Concepts, Jan was a partner in a Winnipeg-based management-consulting firm. She has also worked in the field of adult learning as a consultant in post-secondary education. She has an ongoing interest in innovation and change, including technological developments and their impact on peoples' lives.

When she is not attending to clients, Jan will be reading and relaxing with family and friends.

Jan Fraser may be reached by telephone at 204-987-7777 or toll free at 1-800-565-0054. Her office e-mail address is jfraser@moneyconcepts.mb.ca.